D1472430

Appliqué
for little ones

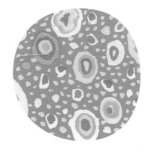

Acknowledgments

I would like to express my heartfelt affection to my sister Brigitte, who introduced me
to appliqué, and to my friend Dominique, for her guidance. I would also like to thank
Le Comptoir at 26 rue Cadet, 75009 Paris for supplying the pretty ribbons, buttons
and braid to decorate my creations.

A DAVID & CHARLES BOOK
Copyright © 2008 by GROUPE FLEURUS
Originally published in France as Appliqué

First published in the UK in 2008 by David & Charles Ltd

David & Charles is an F+W Media Inc. company
4700 East Galbraith Road
Cincinnati, OH 45236

A CIP catalogue record for this book is available from the
British Library.

ISBN-13: 978-0-7153-3209-2 paperback
ISBN-10: 0-7153-3209-0 paperback
For Fleurus

Project editor: Christophe Savouré
Editor: Christine Hooghe
Creative director: Laurent Quellet
Art director: Chloé Eve
Layout: idbleu
Stylist: Sophie Mutterer
Illustrations: Sylvie Blondeau
Editorial contributor and templates: Marie Pieroni
Mock-ups: Florence Bellot

Printed in China by R R Donnelley
for David & Charles
Brunel House   Newton Abbot   Devon

Visit our website at www.davidandcharles.co.uk

David & Charles books are available from all good bookshops;
alternatively you can contact our Orderline on 0870 9908222 or
write to us at FREEPOST EX2 110, D&C Direct, Newton
Abbot, TQ12 4ZZ (no stamp required UK only); US customers
call 800-289-0963 and Canadian customers call 800-840-5220.

Appliqué
for little ones

Sylvie Blondeau

with photographs by Jean-Michel Thirion

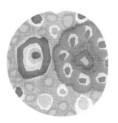

D&C
David and Charles
www.mycraftivity.com

Contents

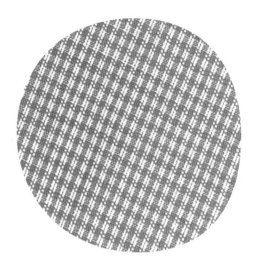

 # Foreword

Appliqué is a fun and straightforward art with endless possibilities. The concept is simple: take small pieces of fabric and sew them on to a background layer. Using this technique, you can create motifs on clothes and accessories, dress rag dolls and make decorative items. Ribbons, braid and embroidered details provide the finishing touches to your designs. This book showcases the technique on a wide variety of items for children, which you can buy or make yourself. In some designs it is used in combination with patchwork backgrounds. Give free rein to your imagination and creativity in all the colours of the rainbow! Let's get sewing!

Fabric and supplies

Beyond fabric and thread, appliqué requires little in the way of equipment. Simply choose any supplies you do buy carefully to make your work effort-free and achieve the best finish.

Essentials

You will need the following equipment to complete the designs in this book.
- Paper for the templates
- Tracing paper (or access to a photocopier)
- Pencil or fabric pencil
- Flat ruler, tape measure
- Paper scissors, dressmaking shears (to cut large pieces), embroidery scissors (to cut small pieces and threads)
- Dressmaker's pins
- Tacking thread
- Assorted sewing needles (see pages 10–11) and embroidery needles (see page 13)
- Iron and ironing board/table

Fabrics. You will find it easiest to work with fine, closely woven cotton fabrics. These fabrics keep their shape while remaining supple and are non-fraying. For these reasons, specialist patchwork fabrics are ideal. Once you are familiar with the techniques involved, you will be able to work with any type of fabric. It is best to wash new fabrics before cutting, to remove coatings that can stiffen them and to allow for shrinkage. In this way you can be confident that your finished piece will be the right size, and you can then wash it without worrying that it will shrink. Pre-washing will also stop your fabrics from shrinking at different rates the first time you wash them and creating unsightly puckered patches in your work. Since appliqué pieces tend to be small, store your offcuts in colour-specific containers ready for your next design.

Thread. Use good quality cotton sewing thread for appliqué and assembly. For your embroidery, you are spoilt for choice. Depending on the effect you want to create, choose from stranded cotton, non-divisible embroidery cotton, perle cotton, soft tapestry cotton, sashiko thread and many more.

Finishing touches. Small details such as ribbons, braid, ric-rac, buttons and beads are all part of the charm of appliqué. The list of materials required for each design includes the decorative touches used in the photographed models. Why not adapt these to suit your taste?

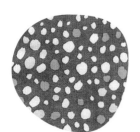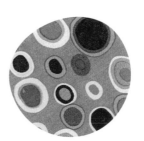

Basic techniques

Spend some time thinking about your choice of fabrics, how the colours will work together and how best to arrange your motifs. Your choice of background fabric is crucial, as it will determine the choice of all your other fabrics. Iron each length of fabric with care before marking out your pieces.

Cutting out. Templates for the appliqué pieces are provided at the back of the book. These are mostly shown to their actual size. Photocopy or trace enough copies to make pieces for the separate elements of a motif (see diagram 1). The dotted lines show the outlines of the pieces under the overlapping sections (see page 11). Cut out the templates, pin them to the right side of your fabric and draw around the outside. Cut the pieces out, adding a 5mm (¼in) seam allowance all the way around (see diagram 2). Do not add a seam allowance to pieces that you intend to machine appliqué using a zigzag stitch or pieces cut from non-fraying fabrics. Clip V-shaped notches up to 1mm ($^{1}/_{16}$in) from the pencil outline along curved sections and at corners (see diagram 3).

The dimensions for square and rectangular pieces are provided in the step-by-step instructions for each design. Mark them out on your fabric and cut them out, adding a 5mm (¼in) seam allowance around the outside.

Be generous when cutting out your background fabric because it will get smaller as you appliqué more pieces on to it. When you have finished your work, you can cut it to the required size.

①

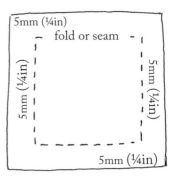

5mm (¼in)
fold or seam
5mm (¼in)   5mm (¼in)
5mm (¼in)

②

③

Before you sew...

Fold the seam allowance around each appliqué piece on to the reverse, wrong sides together, and mark the fold with your nail. Where you have a motif made up of several parts, make sure that the pieces fit together or overlap each other correctly. To mark the fold more cleanly, press with an iron. Lay all your pieces out the way they will look on your finished design, take a step back and make sure that you are happy with the arrangement.

Padding.
Some appliqué pieces, such as faces, can be padded out with wadding to add relief. Use polyester wadding designed for quilting. Using the template as a guide, cut the wadding out without adding a seam allowance. Place it in the centre of the piece on the back of the fabric and fold the seam allowance over the top.

Achieving the perfect circle

Take a piece of card and cut out a template to your desired diameter. Sew a gathering thread (see page 12) around your fabric circle 2mm (1/8in) from the edge. Place the template on the back of your fabric in the centre and pull the thread so the fabric is pulled over the card. Iron the fold. Remove the template and undo the stitching.

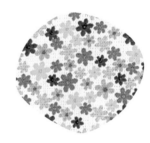

Tips

• On appliqué pieces, mark out your seam allowance on the right side of the fabric. On other pieces, mark out the allowance on the back of the fabric.

• Be sure to place non-symmetrical pieces the right way around on your fabric.

• When working on a design comprising several pieces stitched together with no background fabric, pin the pieces to a length of butter muslin. Butter muslin is a fine cloth with an open weave that works well as a support fabric and will not be seen under your finished work.

Hand appliqué.

Work with short, very fine sewing needles. These will give you greater control over your stitching and will not leave marks in your fabric. Ensure that the seam allowance is folded cleanly on to the back of the fabric all the way around the piece you want to appliqué. Pin the piece to the right side of your background fabric. Thread a needle with sewing thread and tie a small knot in the end. Insert the needle from behind, go through all the layers of fabric and bring it out on top of the appliqué piece, as close to the edge as possible (A). Go back through the background fabric level with the appliqué piece to create a small diagonal stitch (B). Pull the thread through from the reverse. Bring the needle out a short way along the appliqué piece (C) and sew another diagonal stitch into the background fabric. Repeat at regular intervals. Try to start your appliqué with a straight line. You can then sew to the right, left, top or bottom, depending on what you feel most comfortable with. When you come to the end of your thread, secure on the reverse with a few small backstitches, one on top of the other.

Machine appliqué.

Fit your sewing machine with a needle appropriate for the thickness of your fabric. Take the time to adjust the tension and the stitch settings, and sew a few test runs on an offcut of fabric if needed.

Pin the appliqué piece to the right side of your background fabric. Place your pins in the centre of the piece so as not to impede the progress of the foot. When sewing very small pieces, use two or three tacking stitches instead. At the start and end of your stitching, run the machine forward and backward carefully to secure the threads.

Running stitch

Fold the seam allowance on to the reverse of the appliqué piece, as for hand appliqué. Sew 1mm ($^1/_{16}$ in) from the edge of the piece.

Zigzag stitch

Your appliqué pieces should have no seam allowance. If the fabric is likely to fray, iron a piece of iron-on fabric or fusible webbing to the reverse before cutting it out. Machine sew level with the edge of the piece, without crossing over on to the background fabric.

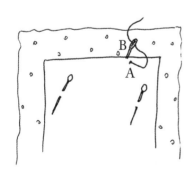

Hand appliqué

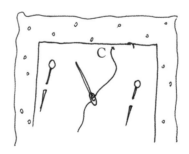

Machine appliqué
(zigzag stitch)

Reverse appliqué. Transfer the motif on to your background fabric and cut it out from the centre, leaving a 5mm (¼in) seam allowance inside the outline you have drawn (diagram 1). Clip notches in the seam allowance and fold it on to the reverse, wrong sides together. Place a piece of fabric behind the background fabric and sew the edges of the hollowed-out motif to the fabric (diagram 2).

① ②

Overlapping

Appliqué motifs are often made up of several pieces. It is important to add these pieces in the right order to add relief and a sense of realism to your designs. To do this, work out how the pieces will fit together in the finished design. In the first example shown here, the legs and arms are sewn on first, followed by the shorts, the shirt and the head. In the second example, however, the dress is sewn on over the neck, the arms and the legs.

Quilting. Quilting is a technique used to add volume to a design. Place your background fabric on top of the lining, wrong sides together, with the wadding in between. Pin the three layers together at regular intervals, making sure there are no creases. Work with a quilting needle (short and sturdy) and quilting thread, sashiko thread or non-divisible embroidery cotton. Sew rows of running stitch (see page 13); space these out at regular intervals from one end of your work to the other or follow a motif. Start each row at the centre and sew one side and then the other. This will allow you to keep a consistent thickness and prevent the fabrics from being pushed to one end. Use enough thread to sew each row without changing. If you do have to change your thread, sew a small backstitch to secure, then thread the end into your work.

Quilting stitch

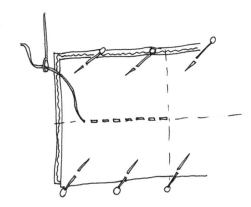

Backstitch

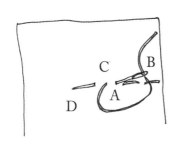

①

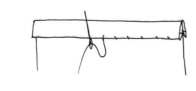

②

Bias binding

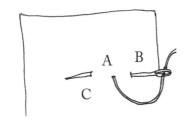

③

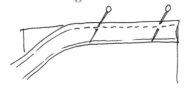

④

Tip

When working on small-scale designs, it is not essential to cut your strips on the bias. Mark them out carefully parallel or perpendicular to the selvage, then follow the instructions on the right.

Assembly.
Place the two pieces you want to sew together one on top of the other, right sides together, and line up the edges and the corners carefully. Sew along the seam line. Work by hand using a backstitch, or by machine with a running stitch.

To assemble patchwork, sew your pieces together in pairs to make strips, then sew the strips together.

Backstitch

Work from right to left, following diagrams 1 and 2. Bring your needle out on the line you want to sew (A). Insert it behind this point (B) and come out again ahead of your starting point (C). Pull the thread through. Now insert your needle at the end of the previous stitch (A) and come out again ahead of your starting point (D). Repeat.

Gathering.
Use this technique to make up some appliqué pieces and add flounces.

Thread a needle with a doubled-up length of sewing thread and tie a knot in the end. Sew a running stitch (see page 13) a few millimetres from the edge all the way along the piece you want to gather. When you reach the end, pull the thread to obtain the desired length and secure with a few small backstitches, one on top of the other. Even out the flounces.

Bias binding.
Bias binding is a strip of border fabric cut on the bias that curves neatly around your work. Bias binding is readily available to buy, but by making your own you can match it perfectly to your creations.

Making your own bias binding

On the reverse of your fabric, mark out parallel strips 2cm (¾in) wide at a 45-degree angle to the selvage. Cut the strips out, then sew them together at each end 1cm (³⁄₈in) from the edges, right sides together. Open out the seam allowances and press with an iron. Fold the edges into the centre lengthways, wrong sides together, and iron the fold. Fold the edges at the centre, mark the fold with your iron, and unfold.

Adding bias binding

Pin the bias binding to your work, right sides together, lining up one of the fold lines with the seam line. Sew along the fold (see diagram 3). Fold the bias binding wrong sides together along the second fold line, pull it over on to the back of your work and pin. Secure with a small slipstitch (see diagram 4).

Embroidery.
The templates provided at the back of the book show the details to be embroidered. You can either copy these on to your fabric or work freehand. Use an embroidery needle with a pointed tip and an eye large enough to accommodate your thread without causing it to jam or fray.

Running stitch
Work from right to left. Your stitches should be the same length as the spaces between them (diagram 1).

Stem stitch
Work from left to right, keeping the thread under the needle as you work (diagram 2).

Threaded running stitch
Sew a row of running stitch. Working from right to left again, weave a second thread under your stitches. To prevent the thread from catching, use a blunt needle. For a highly decorative effect, use a thicker thread in a different colour for the threaded stitch (diagram 3).

French knot
The French knot is used first and foremost for adding eyes. Wind the thread around your needle several times. The more you wind, the larger the knot. Keeping the thread taut in your left hand, put the needle back through the fabric (diagram 4).

Blanket stitch
This stitch is used to reinforce edges. Work from left to right. Change the height of the stitches to suit your needs (diagram 5).

Tip
Backstitch (see opposite) is another useful embroidery stitch.

Hair
Wind up a skein of soft tapestry cotton or fine wool. Secure it to the top of the head in the centre with a few tight stitches. Secure the hair in the same way on either side of the face. Create the hairstyle of your choice: fringe, bunches, plaits or buns. Where needed, hold the hairstyle in place with a few discreet stitches. Even up the strands. To make frizzy hair, embroider large French knots very close together.

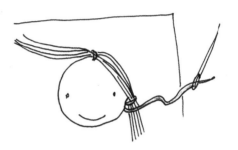

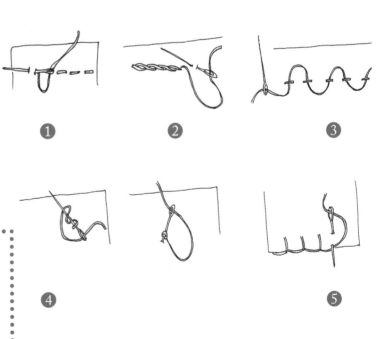

❶   ❷   ❸

❹   ❺

All things girly

Pretty in pink! From cushions dotted with hearts to a doll's house packed with tiny details, girls will love these pieces, designed with only them in mind.

My favourite cushion

Techniques required

Hand appliqué, reverse motifs, patchwork, machine assembly

Size

60 x 60cm (24 x 24in) (excluding flounce)

Materials required

- Fabric for centre panel and flounce: 90 x 75cm (35½ x 29½in)
- Printed fabrics for the patchwork and the dresses: photographed model uses 8 different fabrics; allow 60 x 20cm (23½ x 8in) for each
- Printed fabric for the centre panel frame: 35 x 10cm (14 x 4in)
- Plain fabrics for the faces: 4 offcuts
- Plain fabric for the back of the cover: 61 x 75cm (24 x 29½in)
- Polyester wadding: 25 x 10cm (10 x 4in)
- Ric-rac braid: 65cm (25½in)
- Ribbons and buttons to decorate the dresses
- Sewing thread in colours to match your fabrics
- Perle and stranded cotton in two different colours for the hearts
- Embroidery cotton to match the face fabrics
- Soft tapestry cotton and stranded cotton for the hair
- 1 cushion 60 x 60cm (24 x 24in)

1 Prepare your materials.

Cut out your three templates: the face and the dress (page 117), and heart no.2 (page 112). Copy four dresses and four faces on to the appropriate pieces of fabric, then cut them out, adding a 5mm (¼in) seam allowance around each piece. Clip notches in the seam allowance and fold on to the reverse, wrong sides together. Cut four faces from your wadding, without adding a seam allowance this time.

2 Reverse hearts.

Mark out four 15 x 15cm (6 x 6in) squares on the fabrics you will use for the patchwork. Cut them out, adding a 5mm (¼in) seam allowance. Draw a heart in the centre of each square on the diagonal, using the template as a guide (see diagram below). Cut the heart out from the centre of the square, leaving a 5mm (¼in) seam allowance inside the outline you have drawn. Clip notches in the seam allowance and fold on to the reverse, wrong sides together. Pin a piece of different fabric underneath, right side up, and appliqué the edge of the hollowed-out heart on to it. Embroider a slightly larger heart around the outside in a threaded running stitch, using stranded cotton for the running stitch and perle cotton for the threaded stitch.

3 Patchwork.
Mark out four 15 x 15cm (6 x 6in) squares and sixteen 7.5 x 7.5cm (3 x 3in) squares. Cut them out, adding a 5mm (¼in) seam allowance around each one. Sew the small squares together in groups of four in a checkerboard pattern with the prints diagonally opposite each other. You should now have four 16 x 16cm (6¼ x 6¼in) squares.

Make up two strips as follows: one heart square, one plain square, one checkerboard, one heart square. Sew another two strips as follows: one checkerboard, one plain square. On each strip, sew a length of ric-rac braid over the join between the plain square and the checkerboard.

4 Centre panel.
Mark out a 30 x 30cm (12 x 12in) square and cut it out, adding a 5mm (¼in) seam allowance all round. Place the girls on top on the diagonals, leaving a gap of at least 3cm (1¼in) around the outside. Appliqué the dresses and then the faces, inserting your wadding between the faces and the fabric. Embroider the arms and the legs in a stem stitch. Use a backstitch to embroider the mouths and a French knot or flat stitch for the eyes. Sew a small horizontal stitch for the noses. Add the hair, varying the hairstyles as you go. Sew a length of ribbon to the bottom of each dress and attach the buttons.

Mark out a large cross in the centre of the panel and, keeping within the 3cm (1¼in) margin, finish each arm of the cross in a heart shape around each girl. Embroider this motif with running stitch.

5 Assembly: front.
Sew your two small patchwork strips to either side of the centre panel, then sew the two large strips to the other sides.

Cut four 35 x 2cm (14 x ¾in) strips from the fabric for the centre panel frame. Pin them around the centre panel, making 45° folds at the ends. Appliqué them with an embroidered running stitch 2mm (⅛in) from the inside edge and then 2mm (⅛in) from the outside edge.

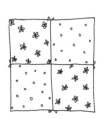

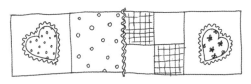

③

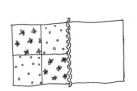

④

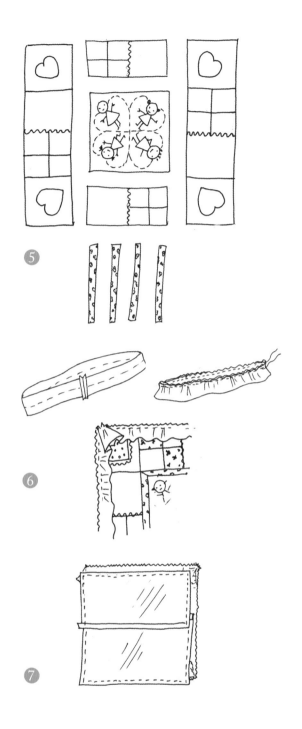

⑤

⑥

⑦

6 Flounce. Cut four 90 x 11cm (35½ x 4½in) strips. Sew them end to end to form a circle. Fold this circle in half lengthways, wrong sides together. Sew a gathering thread all the way along the open sides 2mm (⅛in) from the edge, going through both layers. Pull the thread to obtain a circumference of 244cm (96in) and secure. Even out the flounces. Tack the flounce to the top of the cushion cover on the right side of the fabric, lining up the gathered edge carefully with the edge of your pieces.

7 Assembly: back. Cut your fabric for the back of the cover into two 61 x 37.5cm (24 x 14¾in) rectangles. On each piece, fold one of the lengths over by 1cm (⅜in) twice, wrong sides together, and hem. Pin the rectangles to the front of the cover, right sides together, on top of the flounce. Position the hemmed edges so that they overlap in the centre of your work. Sew the four sides 5mm (¼in) from the edges. Turn the cover out and insert your cushion.

Tips

• Use the patterns in your fabrics to add interest to your design. In the photographed model, we have used the same fabric for one of the hearts (framing a large flower) and the dress of the girl at bottom left of the picture on page 15 (an area of the pattern with small flowers).

• For a neater finish on the centre panel frame, fold the edges of the strips over by 5mm (¼in), wrong sides together, before sewing them on. Your original strips should be 3cm (1¼in) wide.

Pretty in pink sports bags

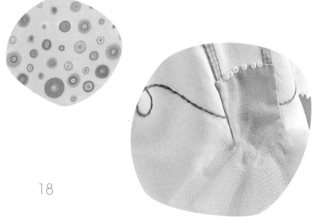

Tip
To make the swim bag waterproof, insert a lining made from a plastic-based material, such as a shower curtain fabric.

Hand appliqué, machine assembly

Size
25 x 28cm (10 x 11in) (excluding handle)

Materials required

BOTH MODELS
- Fabric for the top section: 54 x 22cm (21¼ x 8¾in)
- Fabric for the bottom section and handle: 50 x 30cm (20 x 12in) (coated fabric for the swim bag)
- Offcut for the appliqué
- Fine cord: 120cm (48in)
- Sewing thread in colours to match your fabrics
- Embroidery cotton

DANCE BAG
- Tulle netting: 20 x 5cm (8 x 2in)
- Offcut of ribbon, 2mm (⅛in) wide
- A few small beads

1 Prepare your materials.
Cut out the template for your chosen item of clothing (page 113) and transfer it on to the appropriate fabric. Cut it out, adding a 5mm (¼in) seam allowance around the outside. Clip notches in the seam allowance and fold it on to the reverse, wrong sides together.

2 Appliqué.
Cut the fabric for the top section into two 27 x 22cm (10⅝ x 8¾in) rectangles. Lay one rectangle out lengthways, right side up. Pin the swimsuit or tutu in the centre, leaving a gap of at least 2cm (¾in) below and at least 5.5cm (2⅛in) at the top. To make the tutu straps, cut two small lengths of ribbon and tuck them a couple of millimetres under the leotard. Appliqué the swimsuit or tutu.

3 Decorative touches.
For the dance bag, gather one of the long edges of your strip of tulle netting until it is the same length as the red line on the template. Appliqué to the leotard. Sew the beads along the neckline.

Embroider drops of water around the swimsuit or a swirl on either side of the tutu in a stem stitch.

4 Handle.
Cut a 50 x 8cm (20 x 3⅛in) strip. Fold it in half lengthways, right sides together. Sew the long sides together 1cm (⅜in) from the edge. Turn your work out. Move the seam so it sits in the centre of one of the sides and iron. If you are using coated fabric, place a cloth between the fabric and the iron.

5 Assembly.
To make the bottom section of the bag, cut out a 27 x 22cm (10½ x 8¾in) rectangle. Assemble it between the two rectangles that make up the top section, sewing 1cm (⅜in) from the edges, right sides together. Fold your work in half, right sides together. Sew the sides together 1cm (⅜in) from the edge, leaving a 1cm (⅜in) gap 3cm (1¼in) from the top edge on each side. Turn your work out.

Fold the top edge over by 1cm (⅜in), wrong sides together, and then over by 2cm (¾in). Thread the ends of the handle under this hem in the centre of each side of the bag. To form a sleeve for your cord, sew around the top edge of the bag, 5mm (¼in) below the openings at the sides. Cut your cord into two pieces of equal length. With the aid of a safety pin, thread one length of cord into the sleeve and all the way around the bag, then tie the ends together on one side. Add the second length of cord in the same way, bringing it out on the other side.

2 3   4   5

My doll's house

House

Techniques required

Hand appliqué, hand assembly

Size

20cm (8in) (width) x 15cm (6in) (depth) x
23cm (9in) (height)

Materials required

• Fabric for exterior walls and floor:
63 x 30cm (25 x 12in)
• Fabric for roof exterior:
34 x 16cm (13½ x 6¼in)
• Fabric for front gable exterior:
21 x 11cm (8¼ x 4½in)
• Fabric for interior: 84 x 38cm (33 x 15in)
 (if using several different fabrics, as in the
 example here, see the table below)
• White fabric for door and windows:
25 x 15cm (10 x 6in)
• Assorted offcuts of fabric for the appliqué
 pieces (including a flesh-coloured fabric)
• Polyester wadding: 145 x 25cm (57 x 10in)
• Acetate film: 1 sheet 50 x 65cm (20 x 25½in)
• Ric-rac braid: 100cm (40in)
• Ribbon for the window bars: 25cm (10in)
• Green silk ribbon for the leaves on the flowers
• 2 large press studs
• For the straps, length of ribbon at least
 as wide as the press studs: 15cm (6in)
• Flower-shaped and butterfly-shaped buttons,
 buttons for the handles, leaf-shaped beads,
 rocaille beads, ribbons, braid, lace
• Sewing thread in colours to match your fabrics
• Embroidery cotton
• Soft tapestry cotton or fine wool for the hair

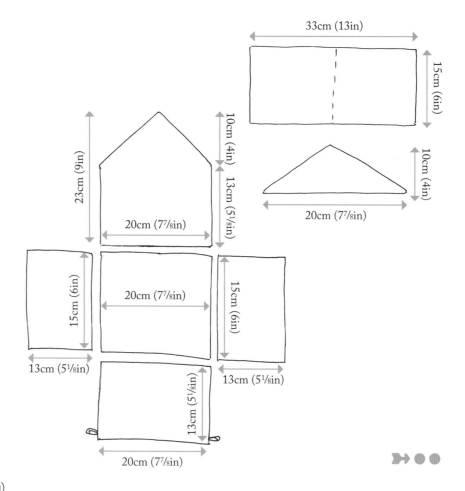

	Finished size	Exterior fabric	Interior fabric	Wadding	Acetate
Floor	20 x 15cm (7⅞ x 6in)	1 x	1 x	1 x	1 x
Side walls	15 x 13cm (6 x 5⅝in)	2 x	2 x	2 x	2 x
Front wall	20 x 13cm (7⅞ x 5 1/8in)	1 x	1 x	1 x	1 x
Rear wall	see diagram	1 x	1 x	1 x	1 x
Front gable	see diagram	1 x	1 x	1 x	1 x
Roof	33 x 15cm (13 x 6in)	1 x	1 x		
	16.5 x 15cm (6½ x 6in)			2 x	2 x

1 Prepare your panels.

Mark out the pieces listed in the table on page 20. Cut them out in the appropriate fabrics, adding a 5mm (¼in) seam allowance around each one. Do not add a seam allowance to your wadding and the acetate pieces.

2 Prepare your appliqué pieces.

Cut out the templates (page 114). Transfer the pieces on to the appropriate fabrics and cut them out, adding a 5mm (¼in) seam allowance around each one. Clip notches in the seam allowances and fold on to the reverse, wrong sides together. Cut the foliage for the two trees from your wadding without adding a seam allowance.

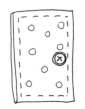

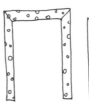

❸ Front wall exterior: door

3 Appliqué.

Follow these instructions to decorate the panels of the house.

Front wall exterior: door. Mark out one 6 x 10cm (2³⁄₈ x 4in) rectangle on your white fabric, one 0.5 x 30cm (¼ x 12in) strip for the door frame and one 6 x 20cm (2³⁄₈ x 8in) rectangle for the door. Cut the three pieces out, adding a 5mm (¼in) seam allowance around each one. Fold the seam allowances on the white fabric and the door frame on to the reverse.

Appliqué the girl to the white rectangle. Sew on the arms and the legs first, followed by the dress, inserting a piece of lace at the bottom between the fabric and the dress, and finally the head. Embroider the facial features and attach the hair.

Fold the door in half widthways, right sides together. Sew the right-hand side and the short open end 5mm (¼in) from the edge. Turn your work out. Embroider a frame through all the layers in a running stitch. Add a button for the handle.

Fold the door frame into an upside down U shape by making 45° corners. Appliqué the white rectangle on top, inserting the open section of the door underneath. Appliqué the door to the wall fabric just above the bottom seam allowance.

Appliqué the flowerpots level with the bottom seam allowance. Embroider a row of running stitch on each one to make the rim, and decorate with buttons and beads. Embroider the stems of the flowers. To make the leaves, embroider a flat stitch in your silk ribbon, then use cotton to embroider a flat stitch in the centre of each leaf for the vein.

Left wall exterior: garden. Appliqué the two trees, positioning them just above the bottom seam allowance. Add the trunks first and then the foliage backed with wadding, overlapping the trunk slightly.

Sew on your butterfly-shaped buttons, then embroider their paths in a running stitch.

Right wall exterior: window. Mark out one 5 x 5cm (2 x 2in) square on your white fabric, one 0.5 x 22cm (¼ x 8¾in) strip for the window frame, and two 6 x 6cm (2³⁄₈ x 2³⁄₈in) squares for the shutters. Cut these four pieces out, adding a 5mm (¼in) seam allowance around each one.

Appliqué two ribbons to your white square in the shape of a cross. Fold back the seam allowance on the window frame and appliqué it around the white square. Work 5mm (¼in) from the edges and make 45° corners. Appliqué the cat, then embroider its nose and eyes.

Fold each shutter in half, right sides together. Sew along the two short ends 5mm (¼in) from the edges. Turn your work out. Embroider a frame and a diagonal line through all the layers in a running stitch. Appliqué the window frame to the wall fabric, inserting the open edge of a shutter underneath on each side.

Decorate the section below the window with flowers. Remember to leave the bottom seam allowance free.

Front gable exterior: dormer window. Mark out a circle 5cm (2in) in diameter on your white fabric. Cut it out, adding a 5mm (¼in) seam allowance around the outside. Appliqué two ribbons to the fabric in the shape of a cross. Fold the edge over by 5mm (¼in), wrong sides together. Appliqué the window to the gable fabric in a running stitch, 2mm (⅛in) from the edge.

Interior walls. Appliqué the furniture to the walls to suit your taste, making sure that you sew the pieces above the bottom seam allowance. Decorate with buttons, braid and embroidered details. To make the picture frame, cut a 3 x 3cm (1¼ x 1¼in) square from a patterned fabric, sew a ribbon around the outside and embroider a picture wire.

 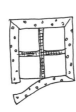   

Right wall exterior: window

4 Straps.

Cut the ribbon for the clasp straps into two pieces of equal length. Sew the stud part of a press stud to one end of each length of ribbon.

5 Assembly.

Take the four front wall pieces. Lay out the interior fabric face down. Place the acetate on top and fold the seam allowance of the fabric over the top. Position one strap on each side approximately 2cm (¾in) from the top edge, with the press stud underneath. Sew the end without the press stud securely to the seam allowance on the fabric. Place the wadding on top of your work. Place the exterior fabric on top, right side up, and fold the seam allowance under the wadding. Sew the two pieces of fabric together with a slipstitch. Use the same technique (without the straps) to assemble the three other walls, the floor and the front gable.

Fold over the seam allowance on the exterior roof fabric, wrong sides together. Pin your ric-rac braid around the outside, on the reverse, so that the waves of the braid overlap the edge of the fabric. Sew it on, sewing through the seam allowance only. Place the interior fabric on top, wrong sides together, with the folded seam allowances one on top of the other. Sew a row down the centre to divide the two sides of the roof. Position your acetate and wadding on each side, working in the same way as for the other panels, then sew the two fabrics together, leaving the waves of the ric-rac braid jutting out between them.

6 Putting the house together.

Work with a slipstitch and a doubled-up length of thread when sewing the house together. Sew the side walls to the short sides of the floor. Sew the front wall to one of the long sides and the rear wall to the other. Sew the side walls to the rear wall. Sew the front gable under the roof. Working from the inside, sew the roof to the top of the walls. Sew the sockets of the press studs to the exterior of the side walls so they meet up with the studs.

Tips

• Before adding the appliqué pieces, ensure that the walls are the right way up. They should be 16cm (6¼in) or 21cm (8¼in) across and 14cm (5½in) high.
• If you cannot get hold of acetate sheets, use plastic office folders.
• The padding and acetate can be replaced with stiff wadding, which you can purchase from haberdasheries and on the internet.
• Sew a ribbon loop in the centre of the roof to make a carry handle for your house.
• To make a mattress or blanket, place two rectangles of fabric one on top of the other, right sides together. Sew three of the sides. Turn the cover right side out and insert a rectangle of wadding or fleece. Fold the open edges on to the inside and close with a slipstitch. Quilt to your taste.

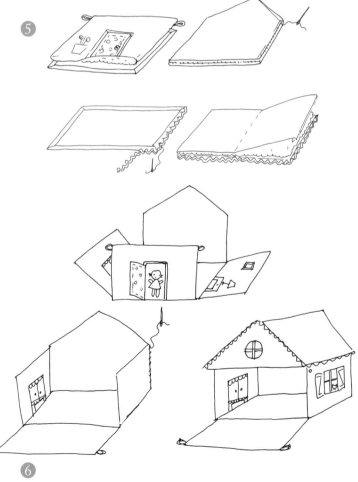

Occupants

Techniques required
Hand appliqué, hand assembly

Size
Height: 8cm (3 ⅛ in)

Materials required
BOTH MODELS
• 2 offcuts, one plain, the other printed
• Polyester wadding
• Sewing thread to match the plain fabric
• Embroidery cotton
DOLL
• Offcut for the cheeks
• Offcut of lace
• Soft tapestry cotton or fine wool for the hair
• Fabric adhesive

1 Prepare your materials.

Cut out the templates for your chosen character (page 114). Transfer the pieces on to the appropriate fabrics: you will need two copies of the body and, for the doll, two copies of the dress. Cut the pieces out, adding a 5mm (¼in) seam allowance around each one. Do not add a seam allowance around the heart because it is too small. If the fabric starts to fray, back it with iron-on fabric or webbing before cutting out. Clip notches in the seam allowances and fold them on to the reverse, wrong sides together.

2 Assembly.
Place the two body pieces one on top of the other, wrong sides together. Sew them together with a slipstitch, stuffing your work with wadding as you go.

3 Decorative touches.

Embroider the eyes and the mouth.
Cat. Appliqué the heart to the stomach using large stitches.
Doll. Sew the sides of the dress together 5mm (¼in) from the edges, right sides together. Sew the lace around the bottom on the reverse. Place the dress on the doll, then appliqué the neckline below the head. Glue on two small circles of fabric for the doll's cheeks. Attach the hair to finish.

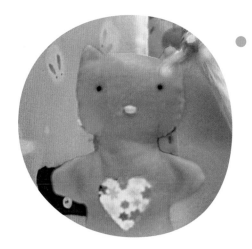

♥ My secret case

Techniques required
Hand appliqué, reverse motifs, quilting,
hand or machine assembly

Size
25 x 15cm (10 x 6in) (folded); 25 x 45cm (10 x 18in) (unfolded)

Materials required
- 3 fabrics for the pocket fronts: 20 x 20cm (8 x 8in) each
- 3 fabrics for the pocket linings: 20 x 20cm (8 x 8in) each
- 3 fabrics for the reverse hearts: 15 x 15cm (6 x 6in) each
- Inner fabric: 25 x 47cm (10 x 18½in)
- Outer fabric: 25 x 47cm (10 x 18½in)
- Fabric for the border and the strap: 90 x 10cm (35½ x 4in)
- Polyester wadding: 25 x 45cm (10 x 17¾in)
- Rocaille beads
- 3 buttons of different diameters
- Sewing thread in colours to match your fabrics
- Perle cotton and fine embroidery cotton

1 Prepare your materials.
Cut out the template for the pocket (page 135) and the template for heart no.2 (page 112). Transfer the pocket on to each of the fabrics for the pocket fronts and linings and cut them out, adding a 5mm (¼in) seam allowance around the outside. Clip notches in the seam allowances.

2 Reverse hearts.
Mark out a heart in the centre of the three pocket fronts, using the template. Cut the heart out, including a 5mm (¼in) seam allowance inside the outline. Clip notches in the seam allowance and fold it on to the reverse, wrong sides together. Pin a piece of fabric intended for the reverse motifs underneath, right side up, and appliqué the edge of the hollowed-out heart to it. Embroider a slightly larger heart around the outside in a threaded running stitch, using fine cotton for the running stitch and perle cotton for the threaded stitch. On the reverse, trim the fabrics of the reverse motifs so they do not show on the pocket fronts.

3 Pockets.
Working right sides together, place each pocket front on to a pocket lining. Sew together 5mm (¼in) from the edge, leaving the bottom open. Turn your work out. Fold the open edges on to the inside by 5mm (¼in) and sew together with a slipstitch.

4 Inside.
Pin the inner fabric to the wadding, leaving 1cm (³⁄₈in) excess fabric at each end. Quilt by sewing five evenly spaced lengthways rows. Embroider swirls to your taste.

Sewing only through the fabric this time, appliqué the pockets, leaving the rounded top sections open. Position one pocket 1cm (³⁄₈in) from the bottom edge and space the other two pockets 1cm (³⁄₈in) apart. You should have 2cm (¾in) remaining at the top. Sew beads around the pockets.

5 Assembly.
Cut a 6 x 4cm (2³⁄₈ x 1½in) strip from the fabric for the strap. Fold the edges over lengthways by 1cm (³⁄₈in), wrong sides together. Now fold the edges one on top of the other and secure with a slipstitch. Fold the strap in half and pin to the inner fabric in the centre of the top edge, with the folded end hanging down. Place the outer fabric on top of the inner fabric, right sides together. Sew the short ends 1cm (³⁄₈in) from the edges, level with the wadding and the bottom pocket. Turn your work out.

Cut two 45 x 4cm (17¾ x 1½in) strips from your border fabric. Fold the edges over lengthways by 1cm (³⁄₈in), wrong sides together, mark the folds and unfold. Sew these strips to the sides of the case using the technique for adding bias binding. At the ends, fold the fabric on to the inside and close the edges with a slipstitch.

Fold the case into three. Sew the three buttons one on top of the other to the outer fabric, opposite the strap.

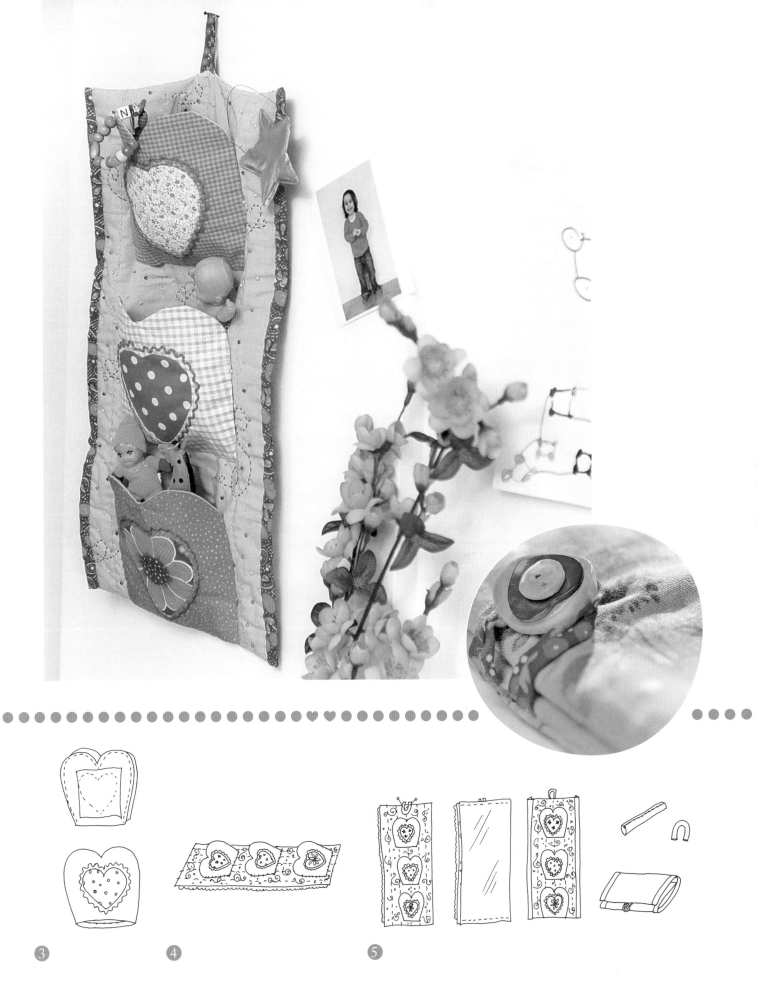

3

4

5

The big goodnight!

Turn bedtime into a pleasure with these cuddly bedroom companions. Sweet dreams!

 Pyjama case

Techniques required

Hand appliqué, hand or machine assembly

Size

Height: 38cm (15in) (excluding legs)

Materials required

BOTH MODELS

- Fabric for the body: 90 x 40cm (35½ x 15¾in)
- Polyester wadding: 30 x 20cm (12 x 8in)
- Flat elastic (5mm/¼in wide): 20cm (8in)
- Ribbon to hang your pyjama case: 20cm (8in)
- 2 buttons for the eyes
- Sewing thread in colours to match your fabrics
- Embroidery cotton for the facial features

GIRL

- Fabric for the hair: 40 x 15cm (15¾ x 6in)
- Offcut of fabric for the cheeks
- Fabrics for the nightdress: 31 x 23cm (12¼ x 9in) for the main section; 31 x 6cm (12¼ x 2 ³/₈in) for the flounce

- Fabric for the slippers: 25 x 10cm (10 x 4in)
- Fabrics for the nightcap: 35 x 10cm (14 x 4in) for the cap; 25 x 6cm (10 x 2 ³/₈in) for the flounce
- Bias binding: 50cm (20in)
- Ric-rac braid: 35cm (14in)
- Raffia for the bunches: 25cm (10in)
- Velvet ribbon for the slippers: 25cm (10in)
- 2 beads for the slippers
- 2 buttons for the nightdress

BOY

- Fabric for the hair: 20 x 10cm (8 x 4in)
- Fabrics for the pyjamas: 50 x 30cm (20 x 12in) for the main sections; 45 x 10cm (18 x 4in) for the collar and pockets
- Fabric for the nightcap: 35 x 30cm (14 x 12in)
- 2 offcuts of felt for the teddy bear
- 4 buttons for the pyjamas
- 2 very small buttons for the teddy bear's eyes

• Both models

1 Prepare your materials.
The templates for this design are provided on page 118. Enlarge them to 200% and cut them out. Transfer them on to the appropriate pieces of fabric, making the number of copies indicated on page 118. Cut the pieces out, adding a 5mm (¼in) seam allowance around each one. Do not add a seam allowance to the teddy bear pieces. Clip notches in the seam allowances. Cut one body from wadding, adding a 5mm (¼in) seam allowance around the outside.

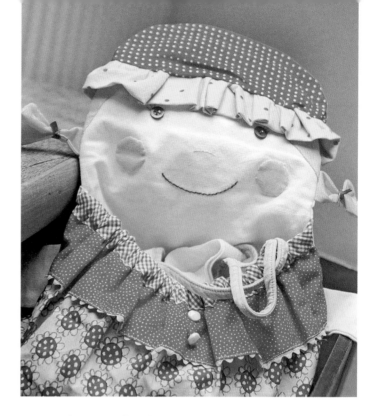

2 Face.
Fold the seam allowance of the hair on to the reverse, wrong sides together, along the red line on the template. Position the hair at the top of one of the body sections and appliqué the folded section to it. Sew on the buttons for the eyes. Embroider the mouth and nose. On the girl, embroider eyelashes and appliqué two small circles of fabric for the cheeks. On the boy, embroider freckles with a French knot. For the boy, continue on page 32.

• Girl

3 Nightdress.
Fold over one side of the flounce lengthways by 5mm (¼in), wrong sides together. Sew ric-rac braid to this hem so the waves overlap. Pin the other side of the flounce to one of the long edges of the main section, wrong side of the flounce against the right side of the main section. Pin the bias binding to this edge, right side of the bias binding against the wrong side of the main

section. Sew 1cm (³⁄₈in) from the edge. Flip the bias binding on to the right side of the flounce and topstitch a few millimetres from the edge. Thread the elastic under the bias binding, adjust it so the neckline is the same width as the body at the green mark on the template, then sew it securely at both ends. Sew the buttons to the flounce.

4 Legs and arms.
Fold a piece of bias binding over the top edge of each slipper and appliqué. Sew a ribbon bow topped with a bead to the bias binding on two of the slippers. Position one slipper at the bottom of each leg, wrong side of the slipper against the right side of the leg, and tack. Place the legs and arms one on top of the other in pairs, right sides together. Sew 5mm (¼in) from the edge, leaving the short straight edge open. Turn your work out.

5 Bunches.
Place the bunches one on top of the other in pairs, right sides together. Sew 5mm (¼in) from the edge, leaving the short straight edge open. Turn your work out.

②

③

④

6 Assembly.

Place the nightdress on the fabric body with the face, wrong side of the nightdress against the right side of the body. Position the arms, legs and bunches as shown in red on the template for the body, lining up the open edges with the edges of the nightdress and the face. Place the front of the slippers decorated with the bow against the nightdress. Position the second fabric body on top, right sides together, followed by the wadding body. Pin all the layers together. Sew 5mm (¼in) from the edges, leaving an opening on one side. Trim the wadding close to the stitching. Turn your work out. Sew up the hole with a slipstitch.

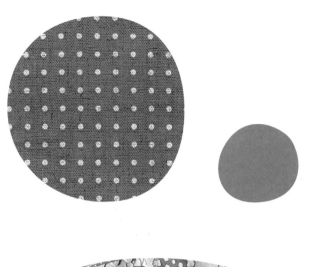

7 Nightcap.

Fold the ribbon to hang your pyjama case in half. Position it on the right side of one of your cap pieces, in the centre at the top, with the folded end hanging down. Place the second cap piece on top, right sides together. Sew 5mm (¼in) from the edges, leaving the bottom edge open. Turn your work out. Fold the bottom edge over by 5mm (¼in), wrong sides together. Fold the flounce in half lengthways, right sides together. Sew the short ends 1cm (³⁄₈in) from the edges. Turn your work out. Sew a gathering thread through both layers along the open side, 2mm (¹⁄₈in) from the edge. Pull the thread until it is 13cm (5in) in length and secure. Even out the flounces. Tack the gathered side to the hem of the cap, centring it at the front, and sew. Place the nightcap on the head and attach it at the level of the flounce. Tie your raffia around the bunches.

5

6

7

• Boy

3 Pyjama shirt. Cut out a 31 x 26cm (12¼ x 10¼in) rectangle. Lay it out lengthways, make a vertical fold at the centre and pin. For the pockets, mark out two 7.5 x 7cm (3 x 2¾in) rectangles. Cut them out, adding a 5mm (¼in) seam allowance around the outside. Fold the seam allowance on to the reverse, wrong sides together. Secure the top seam allowance with a topstitch or embroider with a running stitch. Pin the pockets to the shirt at least 1cm (⅜in) from the bottom edge. Appliqué the two sides and the bottoms of the pockets.

4 Teddy bear. Embroider the mouth on the muzzle and appliqué to the head. Sew on the eyes. Appliqué the stomach to the body. Insert the bottom of the body under one of the pyjama pockets. Appliqué the body and the head, inserting the ears underneath, pinched at their base. Lastly, appliqué the paw, positioning it so that it sits on top of the pocket.

5 Collar. Place the collar pieces one on top of the other in pairs, right sides together. Sew 5mm from the edges, leaving the straight edge open. Turn your work out. Fold the edges of the opening over by 5mm (¼in), wrong sides together, and sew with a slipstitch. Pin the collar pieces to the shirt either side of the centre fold, 3cm (1¼in) from the top edge, with the points pointing upwards. Sew along the straight sides.

Fold the top edge of the shirt over by 1cm (⅜inn) and then 2cm (¾in), wrong sides together. Sew a topstitch 1.5cm (½in) from the top edge. Thread the elastic into the sleeve you have created, adjust it so the neckline is the same width as the body at the green mark on the template, then sew it securely at both ends. Fold the collars back over the shirt. Sew on the buttons.

6 Legs and arms. Place the leg and arm pieces one on top of the other in pairs, right sides together. Sew 5mm (¼in) from the edges, leaving the short straight side open. Turn your work out. To make the sleeves and trousers, cut four 13 x 8.5cm (5 x 3 ⅜in) rectangles. Fold them in half widthways, right sides together. Sew the long edges 5mm (¼in) from the sides. Turn the work out. Fold the bottom edge over by 5mm (¼in), wrong sides together, and secure with a topstitch or embroider in a running stitch. Insert the arms and legs into the cases you have made.

7 Assembly. Follow the instructions for the girl pyjama case (step 6, page 31).

8 Nightcap. Fold the ribbon to hang your pyjama case in half. Position it on the right side of one of your cap pieces, just below the tip on one side, with the folded end towards the inside. Place the second cap piece on top, right sides together. Sew 5mm (¼in) from the edges, leaving the bottom edge open. Turn your work out. Fold the bottom edge over by 5mm (¼in), wrong sides together. Place the cap on the head and sew it on. Fold the tip of the cap so that it hangs to the front and secure with a few stitches.

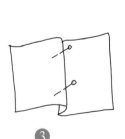 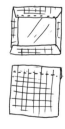 

③

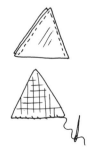 

⑤

Bedroom curtain

Size
Dependent on the size of your sheet

Materials required

- 1 old cot sheet
- Characters cut from reproduction 1930s/1950s fabrics
- Assorted polka dot fabrics
- Fine iron-on fabric
- Gingham ribbon in two colours: 35cm (14in) for each curtain tie (or more depending on the diameter of your curtain pole)
- Buttons: 1 per tie
- Embroidery cotton in colours to match your fabrics and buttons

1 Prepare your materials.
Back your fabrics with iron-on fabric, then cut out squares and rectangles of varying sizes of between 3cm (1¼in) and 8cm (3¼in).

2 Appliqué. Appliqué the pieces to the sheet with a blanket stitch. Sew them on at random intervals, overlapping them occasionally.

3 Ties. Cut curtain ties 35cm (14in) in length from your ribbons. Fold them in half. Attach them to the top of your curtain by sewing a button on to each one. Place one tie at each end, then space the remaining ties at regular intervals (approx. 10cm/4in, depending on the width of the sheet).

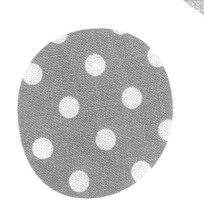

Tip
Why not base your choice of fabrics around a different theme, such as animals or flowers?

Lily and her basket

Asleep/awake doll

Techniques required
Hand appliqué, hand or machine assembly

Size
Height: 38cm (15cm)

Materials required
- Fabric for the body: 70 x 20cm (27½ x 8in)
- Fabric for the dress: 35 x 25cm (14 x 10in)
- Fabric for the hair: 50 x 15cm (20 x 6in)
- Offcut of patterned fabric
- Ribbon 3mm (⅛ in) wide: 40cm (16in)
- Sewing thread in colours to match your fabrics
- Embroidery cotton for the eyes and mouth
- Polyester wadding

1 Prepare your materials.
Cut out the templates (pages 124–125). Transfer the pieces on to the appropriate fabrics, making the number of copies indicated. Cut the pieces out, adding a 5mm (¼in) seam allowance around each one. Mark out two 4 x 4cm (1½ x 1½in) squares on your offcut of patterned fabric. Cut them out, adding a 5mm (¼in) seam allowance around each one. Fold this seam allowance on to the reverse, wrong sides together. Appliqué one square to each dress.

2 Head. On one of the heads, embroider French knots for the eyes and a smiling mouth in a stem stitch. On the other head, embroider closed eyes and a small mouth in a stem stitch. Place the two heads one on top of the other, right sides together. Sew them together 5mm (¼in) from the edge, leaving the base of the neck open. Turn your work out and stuff the head.

3 Arms and legs. Place the arms and legs on top of each other in pairs, right sides together. Sew them together 5mm (¼in) from the edges, leaving the short straight side open. Turn the work out and stuff.

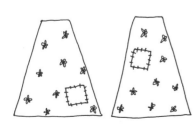

①

②

③

4 Assembly. Position the arms and the legs on one of the dress pieces as indicated in red on the template for the body, lining up the open edges with the edges of the dress. Place the other dress piece on top, right sides together. Pin all the layers together. Sew 5mm (¼in) from the edges, leaving the neckline open. Turn your work out. Fold the edge of the neckline over on to the inside by 5mm (¼in) and stuff. Insert the neck into the neckline and sew with a slipstitch.

5 Hair. Place the two hair pieces one on top of the other, right sides together. Sew 5mm (¼in) from the edge. Turn out. Fold the open edges over by 5mm (¼in), wrong sides together.

Place the bunches one on top of the other in pairs, right sides together. Sew 5mm (¼in) from the edge, leaving the short straight edge open. Turn your work out.

Place the hair on the head of the doll. Insert the open edges of the bunches underneath and appliqué the hair to the head. Tie a ribbon around each of the bunches.

Basket

Techniques required

Hand appliqué, hand or machine assembly

Size

33cm (13in) (length) x 19cm (7½in) (width) x 10cm (4in) (height)
(excluding handles)

Materials required

- Fabric for the outside and the handles: 110 x 35cm (43½ x 14in)
- Fabric for the lining: 110 x 35cm (43½ x 14in)
- Fabrics for the appliqué pieces: 2 offcuts
- Polyester wadding: 105 x 30cm (41½ x 12in)
- Wide braid: 24cm (9½in) (if using embroidered braid, 2 x 12cm (4¾in) pieces, with the motifs in the centre of each piece)
- Scalloped braid: 95cm (37½in)
- Sewing thread in colours to match your fabrics
- Embroidery cotton

1 Prepare your materials.

Cut out the templates for the birds and their wings (page 125). On one of your offcuts of fabric, make two copies of each bird. Repeat on the other offcut for the wings. Cut out the pieces, adding a 5mm (¼in) seam allowance around each one. Fold this seam allowance on to the reverse, wrong sides together. In your outer fabric, mark out one 33 x 19cm (13 x 7½in) rectangle for the base, one 104 x 10cm (41 x 4in) rectangle for the side and two 3.5 x 25cm (1 ⅜in x 10in) strips for the handles. Cut out these four pieces, adding a 1cm (⅜in) seam allowance around each one. Cut one base and one side piece of the same size from your lining fabric and, without adding a seam allowance, from your wadding.

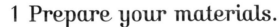

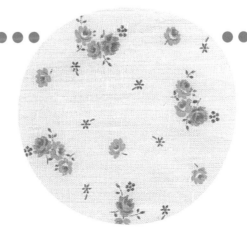

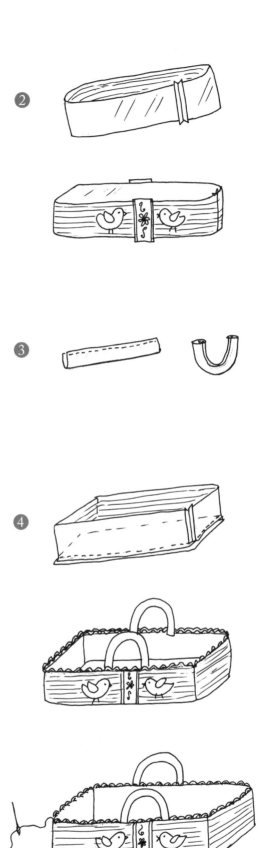

2 Outer sides. Sew the side piece into a
circle by sewing the short ends together 1cm (³/8in)
from the edges, right sides together. Turn your
work out. Cut your wide braid into two pieces of
equal length. Appliqué them vertically in the centre
of the two long sides of the side piece. To work out
where they should go, work on the premise that the
seam will be positioned in one corner of the basket.
Appliqué one bird on either side of each length of
braid. Add the body first, then the wing. Embroider
the eye, beak and feet.

3 Handles. Fold each handle in half
lengthways, right sides together. Sew the long ends
1cm (³/8in) from the edge. Turn your work out.

4 Assembly. Sew the side piece around
the base, right sides together, sewing 1cm (³/8in)
from the edges. To make the lining, sew the side
piece into a circle and sew it around the base in the
same way as for the outer section. Fold over the top
edge of the lining and the outer section by 1cm
(³/8in), wrong sides together. Sew the wadding side
piece into a circle by sewing the short ends to each
other with a few large, loose stitches. Assemble the
base in the same way. Pin the scalloped braid to the
hem of the top edge around the outer side piece.
Pin the handles in the centre of the sides, behind
the braid. Place the wadding side piece inside the
outer section. Add the lining and tuck the wadding
side piece under the hem. Line up the top edges
and sew together with a slipstitch.

Duvet

Techniques required
Hand appliqué, hand or machine assembly

Size
25 x 25cm (10 x 10in)

Materials required
- Main fabric: 27 x 22cm (10¾ x 8¾in)
- Facing: 27 x 7cm (10¾ x 2¾in)
- Fabric for the lining: 27 x 27cm (10¾ x 10¾in)
- Polyester wadding: 27 x 27cm (10¾ x 10¾in)
- Wide braid: 27cm (10¾in) (if using embroidered braid, ensure that the motifs are centred)
- Sewing thread in colours to match your fabrics

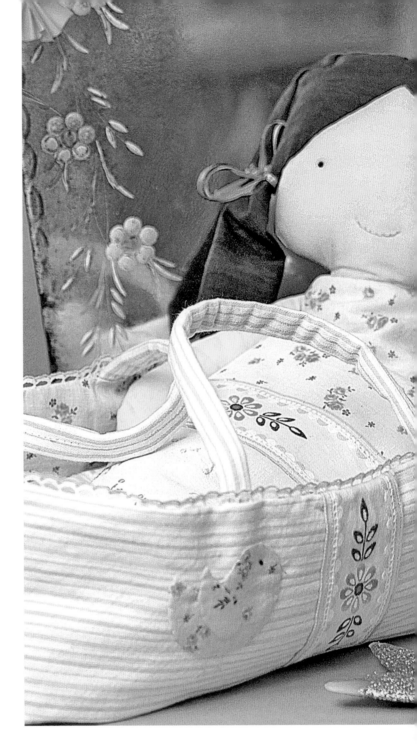

1 Front. Sew the facing to the top of your main fabric, right sides together, sewing 1cm (³⁄₈in) from the edge. Appliqué the braid to the right side so that it sits over the join between the two pieces.

2 Assembly. Lay the main fabric out on the wadding, right side up. Place the lining on top, right sides together. Sew around the outside 1cm (³⁄₈in) from the edge, leaving an opening on one side. Trim the wadding close to the seams and turn your work out. Fold the edges of the opening 1cm (³⁄₈in) on to the inside and sew them together with a slipstitch.

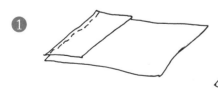

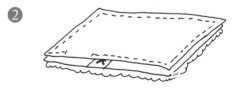

New baby

Welcome baby into the world with these great gift ideas. As charming as they are useful, they are easily customized to suit mother's taste.

 ## Toy tidy

Techniques required
Hand appliqué, hand or machine assembly

Size
46 x 33cm (18 x 13in)

Materials required
- Fabric for the main section: 48 x 22cm (19 x 8¾in)
- Fabric for the pockets: 48 x 27cm (19 x 10¾in)
- Assorted offcuts of fabric for the appliqué pieces (including a flesh-coloured fabric)
- Polyester wadding: 25 x 25cm (10 x 10in)
- Ric-rac braid: 135cm (53in)
- Buttons: 2 for the car wheels, 6 to hang the pockets
- 7 beads or small buttons
- Sewing thread in colours to match your fabrics
- Embroidery cotton
- Soft tapestry cotton or fine wool for the hair

1 Prepare your materials.
Cut out the templates (page 119). Transfer them on to the appropriate fabrics (make three copies of the building block). Mark out one 10 x 9cm (4 x 3½in) rectangle and three circles 2.5cm (1in) in diameter for the bag of marbles. Cut out all the pieces, adding a 5mm (¼in) seam allowance around each piece. Clip notches in the seam allowances and fold them on to the reverse, wrong sides together. Cut the body and the head of the child and the bear from your wadding, without adding a seam allowance.

2 Appliqué: main section.
Embroider the eyes, nose and mouth on to the child's face. Appliqué the child to the main section: add the legs first, followed by the body backed with wadding, then the head, also backed with wadding, and the shoes. Sew on the buttons. Add the hair and embroider the arms. Appliqué the building blocks, overlapping them as you go, then embroider their edges. Embroider the bear's mouth on to the muzzle, appliqué the muzzle to the head and sew the eyes. Appliqué the pads to the end of the paws. Appliqué the bear to the main section: add the front legs and the right hind leg first, followed by the body backed with wadding, then the left hind leg and, lastly, the head backed with wadding, positioning the ears behind, pinched at their base.

3 Appliqué: pockets.

Cut the fabric for the pockets into three 16 x 27cm (6¼ x 10¾in) rectangles. Fold each rectangle in half widthways, wrong sides together. Mark the fold with pins and unfold. Position your appliqué pieces in the top half, leaving a gap of at least 2cm (¾in) around the outside. Embroider the rabbit's nose and sew the eyes before appliquéing it to the fabric. Appliqué the car, then sew on two buttons for the wheels. To make the bag of marbles, appliqué the three circles to the rectangle, overlapping them as you go. Gather the top of the bag by sewing a cord made from embroidery cotton through it in a running stitch, and appliqué.

4 Assembly.

Fold the four sides of the main section over by 5mm (¼in) twice, wrong sides together, and hem. On the right side of the fabric, sew your ric-rac braid around the edge of the piece. Sew six buttons along the bottom edge. Sew the first 3cm (1¼in) from one edge, then space the remaining buttons out at alternate intervals of 10cm (4in) and 5cm (2in). Fold each pocket in half widthways, right sides together. Sew the sides 1cm (³⁄₈in) from the edges. Fold the top edge over by 5mm (¼in) twice, wrong sides together, and hem. Turn your work out. On the back of each pocket, make a strap from thick embroidery cotton 2cm (¾in) from each side, sewing under the hem. Make two more straps on the back of the main section, on the top hem. Place a pole through these straps to hang your toy tidy. Attach the pockets to the buttons on the main section.

Baby's first bag

Techniques required
Hand appliqué, machine assembly

Size
23 x 26cm (9 x 10¼in) (excluding handle)

Materials required
- Fabric for the top section: 50 x 15cm (20 x 6in)
- Fabric for bottom section and handle: 45 x 45cm (17¾ x 17¾in)
- Offcuts of fabric for the appliqué pieces
- 2 buttons
- Flat elastic 5mm (¼in) wide: 25cm (10in)
- Sewing thread in colours to match your fabrics

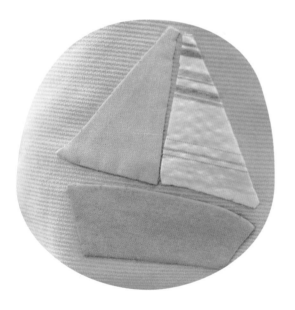

1 Prepare your materials.
Cut out the templates (page 117). Transfer the pieces on to the appropriate fabrics. Cut the pieces out, adding a 5mm (¼in) seam allowance around each one. Clip notches in the seam allowances, then fold them on to the reverse, wrong sides together.

2 Appliqué.
Cut a 25 x 32cm (10 x 12½in) rectangle to make the bottom section of the bag. Fold it in half widthways, wrong sides together. Pin the appliqué pieces to the front, ensuring that you leave a 1cm (³⁄₈in) gap at the top and sides for the seams, then unfold the fabric. Appliqué the boat and car. Appliqué the windows on the car, then sew on the buttons for the wheels.

3 Handle.
Cut a 45 x 12cm (17¾ x 4¾in) strip. Fold it in half lengthways, right sides together. Sew the long sides together 1cm (³⁄₈in) from the edge. Turn your work out. Move the seam to the centre of one of the sides and then iron.

4 Assembly.
Cut the fabric for the top section into two 25 x 15cm (10 x 6in) rectangles. Attach them to either side of the bottom section of the bag, sewing 1cm (³⁄₈in) from the edges, right sides together. Fold the resulting strip in half, right sides together. Sew the sides together 1cm (³⁄₈in) from the edges. Turn your work out. Fold the top edge over by 1cm (³⁄₈in), then 2cm (¾in), wrong sides together. Insert the ends of the handle under this hem in the centre of the two sides of the bag. Topstitch 1.5cm (⁵⁄₈in) from the top edge, leaving a small opening at the end. With the aid of a safety pin, thread the elastic into the hem you have created, then sew the ends together securely. Sew up the hole.

②

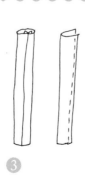
③

④

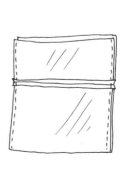

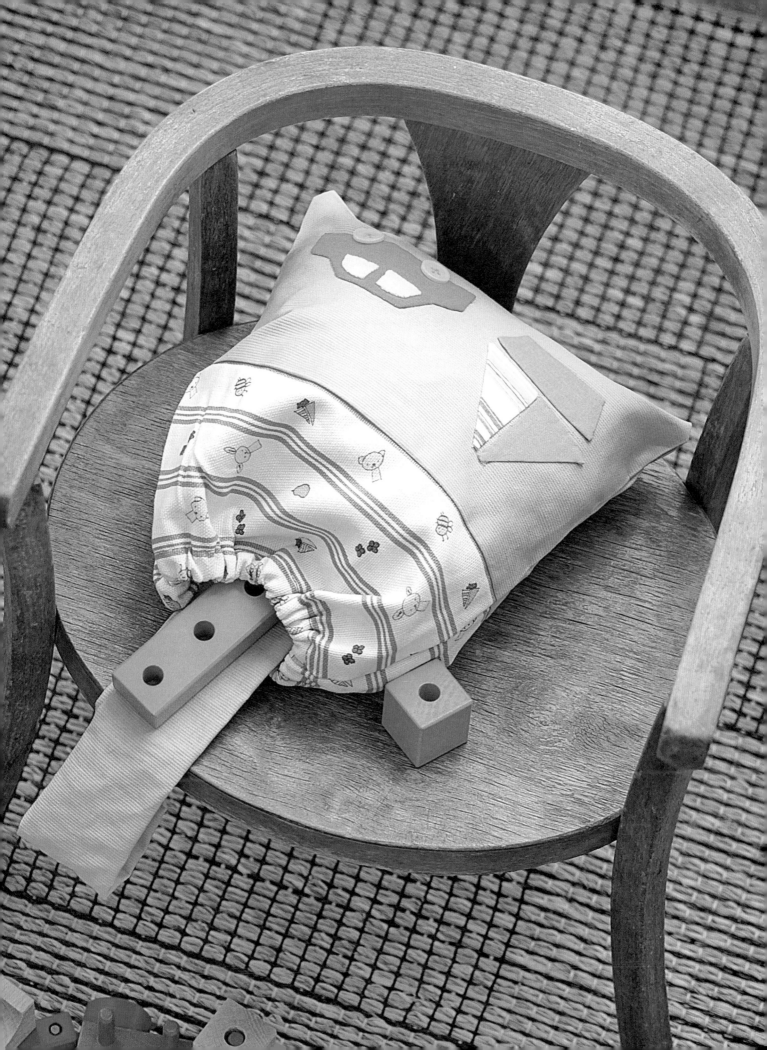

Bonnet and bootee set

Bonnet

Techniques required
Hand appliqué, machine assembly

Size
Head circumference: 53cm (21in)

Materials required
- Wool felt: 75 x 15cm (29½ x 6in)
- Fabrics for the lining: 65 x 15cm (25½ x 6in) for the cap; 15 x 10cm (6 x 4in) for each of the two earflaps
- Offcuts of fabric for the appliqué pieces
- 2 ribbons, each 40cm (15¾in) long
- Sewing thread to match the felt
- Embroidery cotton

1 Prepare your materials.
Cut out the two templates (page 123). Mark out four cap quarters and two earflaps on your felt and your lining fabrics. Cut the pieces out, adding a 1cm (³⁄₈in) seam allowance around each one. Mark out circles 3cm (1¼in) and 5cm (2in) in diameter on your offcuts of fabric. Cut them out, adding a 5mm (¼in) seam allowance around each one. Clip notches in the seam allowances and fold them on to the reverse, wrong sides together.

2 Assembly.
Sew the four felt cap quarters together 1cm (³⁄₈in) from the edges, right sides together. Open out the seam allowances and press with an iron. Position one felt earflap and one fabric earflap one on top of the other, right sides together, placing a ribbon between them. Sew the curved section 1cm (³⁄₈in) from the edge. Turn your work out. Make up the second earflap in the same way. Pin the earflaps on either side of the cap, felt against felt, centring them on the seams. Sew 5mm (¼in) from the edge.

3 Appliqué.
Appliqué circles to each quarter of the cap with embroidery cotton, overlapping them to your taste. Alternate between a slipstitch and a blanket stitch.

4 Lining.
Sew your fabric cap quarters together 1cm (³⁄₈in) from the edges, right sides together, leaving a gap in the centre of one of the seams. Open out the seam allowances and press with an iron. Place the fabric cap on to the felt cap, over the earflaps, and match up the seams. Sew the bottom 1cm (³⁄₈in) from the edge. Turn your work out. Fold the edges around the opening 1cm (³⁄₈in) on to the inside and sew together with a slipstitch. Embroider around the base of the cap and the earflaps in a running stitch, 3mm (¹⁄₈in) from the edge.

Tip
Tie the earflaps on top of the bonnet or let them hang down over baby's ears in cold weather. Choose a ribbon that is wide enough not to injure the child's neck.

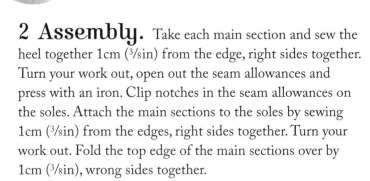

Bootees

Techniques required
Hand appliqué, machine assembly

Size
Birth to 3 months

Materials required
• Wool felt: 50 x 15cm (20 x 6in)
• Fabric for the lining: 50 x 15cm (20 x 6in)
• Offcuts of fabrics for the appliqué pieces
• Sewing thread to match the felt
• Embroidery cotton

1 Prepare your materials.

Cut out the two bootee templates (page 123). Mark out two copies of each piece on your felt, making mirror images of the sole. Mark out identical pieces on the fabric for the lining. Cut out all the pieces, adding a 1cm (3/8in) seam allowance around each one. Make cuts in the main sections, as shown on the template. Mark out circles of varying diameters on your offcuts of fabric. Cut them out, adding a 5mm (1/4in) seam allowance around each circle. Clip notches in the seam allowances and fold them on to the reverse, wrong sides together.

2 Assembly.

Take each main section and sew the heel together 1cm (3/8in) from the edge, right sides together. Turn your work out, open out the seam allowances and press with an iron. Clip notches in the seam allowances on the soles. Attach the main sections to the soles by sewing 1cm (3/8in) from the edges, right sides together. Turn your work out. Fold the top edge of the main sections over by 1cm (3/8in), wrong sides together.

3 Appliqué.

Alternating between slipstitch and blanket stitch, appliqué the circles to the felt main sections using embroidery cotton.

4 Lining.

Sew the fabric pieces together using the same technique as for the felt pieces. Insert the fabric bootees into the felt bootees, wrong sides together. Pin the top edges together and sew with an embroidered running stitch.

1   2   3 4

Sleep tight, baby!

Whether sleeping through the night or taking a quick nap, baby will never be far from the comfort of these delightful designs in cosy fabrics with their welcoming appliquéd friends.

 ## Quilted cushion-blanket

Techniques required
Hand appliqué, quilting, machine assembly

Size
35 x 35cm (14 x 14in) (folded);
105 x 105cm (41 x 41in) (unfolded)

Materials required
- Fabrics for the patchwork: 11 squares 37 x 37cm (14½ x 14½in)
- Fleece for the lining: 107 x 107cm (42 x 42in)
- Offcuts of fabric for the appliqué pieces
- Bias binding: 37cm (14½in)
- Sewing thread in colours to match your fabrics
- Embroidery cotton

1 Prepare your materials.
Cut out the templates for the dog (page 116). Transfer the pieces on to the appropriate fabrics and cut them out, adding a 5mm (¼in) seam allowance around each one. Clip notches in the seam allowances and fold them on to the reverse, wrong sides together. On the reverse of each fabric square, mark out seam lines 1cm (³/₈in) from the edges.

2 Appliqué. Appliqué the dog to the centre of one of your squares of fabric. Add the paws first, then the tail and the dog's left ear, the body and the head, and then the coat and the dog's right ear. Lastly, add the nose, tongue and spots. Embroider the eyes, mouth and the small white, shiny patch on the nose.

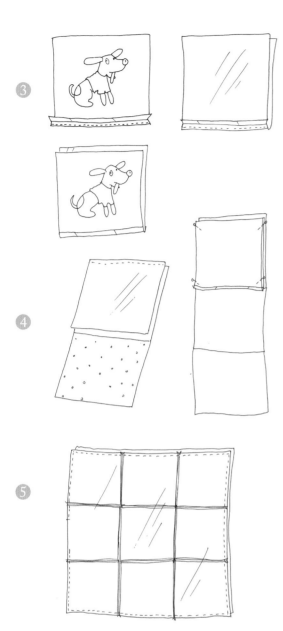

and the bias binding at the bottom. Sew the three strips together 1cm (³⁄₈in) from the edges, right sides together.

5 Assembly.
Place your patchwork on top of the fleece, right sides together. Sew the four sides together, leaving an opening on one side. Turn your work out. Fold the edges of the hole on to the inside by 1cm (³⁄₈in) and sew together with a slipstitch.

6 Quilting.
Embroider a cross at the intersections between the squares in your patchwork. Sew through all the layers to hold the fabrics in place. Store the blanket by folding it into three on the reverse one way and then the other way, and place in the cover.

3 Cover.
Pin one of the sides of the bias binding along the bottom of the square with the dog, right sides together, and sew 1cm (³⁄₈in) from the edge. Fold the bias back over the seam allowance. Pin the other side to a fabric square, right sides together, and sew 1cm (³⁄₈in) from the edge. Turn your work out.

4 Patchwork.
Make up three vertical strips of three squares by sewing them together 1cm (³⁄₈in) from the edges, right sides together. Pin the cover to the top square of your middle strip on the right side of the fabric, with the side without the dog facing up

Tip
The dog motif lends itself well to materials such as felt and fake fur. In the photographed model, we have used thick felt for the tongue (impossible for even the keenest of tiny hands to pull off!). Do not add a seam allowance to synthetic or wool felt pieces. For fake fur, add a seam allowance of a couple of millimetres to give your pieces a neat outline (fold it on to the reverse as you appliqué).

Patchwork cot liner

Techniques required
Hand appliqué, patchwork, quilting,
hand or machine assembly

Size
200 x 42cm (78¾ x 16½in)

Materials required
• Fabric for the centre panel: 52 x 42cm (20½ x 16½in)
• Fabrics for the patchwork: 60 squares 12 x 12cm (4¾ x 4¾in)
• Fabric for the lining: 200 x 42cm (78¾ x 16½in)
• Offcuts of fabrics for the appliqué pieces
• Polyester wadding: 200 x 42cm (78¾ x 16½in) for the padding;
  35 x 15cm (14 x 6in) for the characters
• Bias binding: 6.5m (7yd)
• Sewing thread in colours to match your fabrics
• Embroidery cotton

1 Prepare your materials.

Cut out the templates (pages 126–127). Transfer
them on to the appropriate fabrics (make two
copies of the rabbit's ears and the cat's ears). Mark
out one heart no.2 and one heart no.3 (page 112).
Mark out four circles 14cm (5½in) in diameter and
one circle 6cm (2 ³/₈in) in diameter. Cut out all the
pieces, adding a 5mm (¼in) seam allowance around
each one. Clip notches in the seam allowances and
fold them on to the reverse, wrong sides together.
Cut the heads of the baby, rabbit and cat from your
wadding, without adding a seam allowance. Cut
four of the squares for the patchwork in two. On
the back of these rectangles, the centre panel and
each of the remaining squares, mark seam lines 1cm
(³/₈in) from the edges.

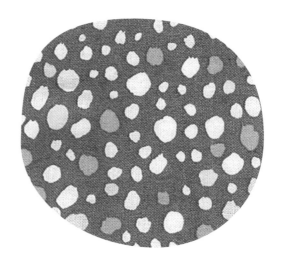

2 Appliqué.

Embroider the baby's head, then appliqué it to the oval piece, backing it with wadding. Unfold the seam allowances on the rabbit's ears and place them one on top of the other in pairs, right sides together. Sew 5mm (¼in) from the edges, leaving the base of the ears open. Turn your work out. Go around the outline of each ear in a running stitch. Embroider the rabbit's head. Back the head with wadding and appliqué it to one of the large circles, sliding the bases of the ears underneath. Secure one of the ears with a few backstitches and leave the other to hang free. Embroider the cat's head, back it with wadding and appliqué to one of the large circles. Sew the ears together in pairs in the same way as for the rabbit. Gather the bases slightly and appliqué. Appliqué heart no.2 to the third large circle, then outline in a running stitch.

3 Secret pocket.

This pocket is the perfect place for a dummy (pacifier). Place the circle with the heart on top of your remaining large circle, right sides together. Sew around the outside 5mm (¼in) from the edge, leaving a small gap. Turn your work out. Fold the edges of the hole 5mm (¼in) on to the inside and sew together with a slipstitch.

4 Centre panel.

Appliqué the secret pocket to the centre panel, leaving the top part open. Appliqué the other motifs, as well as heart no.3 and the small circle. Outline each motif in a running stitch.

5 Patchwork.

Make up eight horizontal strips of seven squares, each ending in a rectangle, by sewing the pieces together 1cm (³⁄₈in) from the edges, right sides together. Assemble the strips in two sets of four.

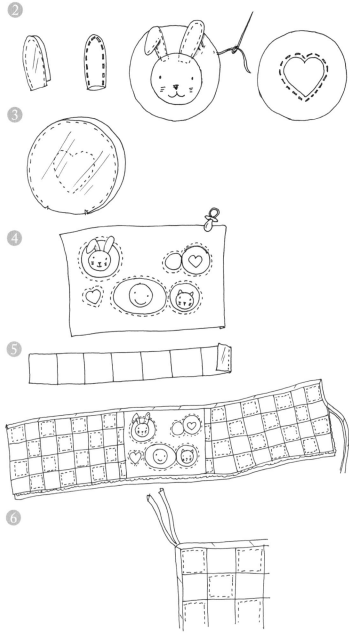

6 Assembly.

Assemble the centre panel between the two pieces of patchwork by sewing the pieces together 1cm (³⁄₈in) from the edges, right sides together. Pin your work to the wadding. In a running stitch, sew around the outline of every other square and rectangle, going through all the layers. Place your work on top of the lining with the wadding against the back of the lining. Add bias binding all the way around. To make the ties, cut your remaining bias binding into eight pieces of equal length. Fold them in half lengthways, wrong sides together, and secure the edges with a slipstitch. Sew the ties to the four corners of your work and at the top and bottom of your rectangles.

Blanket bag

Techniques required
Hand appliqué, hand or machine assembly

Size
21 x 29cm (8¼ x 11½in)

Materials required
- Fleece (or other soft fabric): 55 x 20cm (21½ x 8in)
- Printed fabric: 45 x 25cm (17¾ x 10in)
- Pink fabric: 30 x 20cm (12 x 8in)
- Pompom braid: 42cm (16½in)
- Fine cord: 120cm (47in)
- Polyester wadding
- Sewing thread to match the colours of your fabrics
- Embroidery cotton

1 Prepare your materials.
Cut out the templates (page 113). Transfer them on to your pink fabric: make two copies of the legs and ears of the large pig and the body of the small pig. Cut all the pieces out, adding a 5mm (¼in) seam allowance around each one. Clip notches in the seam allowances. Fold them on to the reverse on the body, head and snout of the large pig and the snout of the small pig, wrong sides together.

2 Appliqué.
Place the legs and ears one on top of the other in pairs, right sides together. Sew 5mm (¼in) from the edges, leaving the straight edge open. Turn your work out. Cut a 44 x 20cm (17½ x 8in) rectangle from your fleece. Fold it in half widthways, wrong sides together. Pin your appliqué pieces to the right side of the fabric, then unfold. Start by appliquéing the body, inserting the legs underneath. Appliqué the snout to the head. Embroider the eyes, nostrils and the mouth. Appliqué the head to the top of the body, inserting the ears underneath. Remember not to appliqué around the arms and ears.

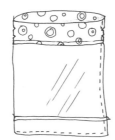

③

⑤

3 Assembly.
Cut one 44 x 18cm (17½ x 7in) strip and one 44 x 5cm (17½ x 2in) strip from your printed fabric. Fold the widest strip in half lengthways, wrong sides together. Working with your fabric right sides together, sew the folded strip to the top of your fleece 1cm (³⁄₈in) from the edges. Sew the other strip to the bottom. Fold your work in half widthways, right sides together. Sew the bottom and the side 1cm (³⁄₈in) from the edges, leaving a 1.5cm (⁵⁄₈in) gap in the side seam 5cm (2in) from the top edge. Turn your work out. On the folded side, cut a buttonhole level with the gap in the seam and embroider with a blanket stitch. Sew a topstitch around the bag on either side of the openings. With the aid of a safety pin, thread your cord twice through the sleeve you have created. Appliqué your braid so that it overlaps the join between the fleece and the top strip.

4 Blanket.
Cut an 8 x 8cm (3 ⅛ x 3 ⅛in) square from an offcut of fleece and go around the outside in a blanket stitch. Place it on the pig, bunch it up slightly and position the pig's leg on top. Secure the leg with a few stitches between the toes.

5 Small pig.
Appliqué the snout to one of the body pieces. Embroider the features on the head. Place the two body pieces one on top of the other, right sides together. Sew 5mm (¼in) from the edges, leaving a gap at the top of the head. Turn your work out. Fold the edges of the gap over by 5mm (¼in) on to the inside and stuff the pig. Thread the ends of the cord into the opening and sew with a slipstitch to secure.

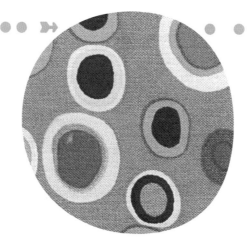

Baby's day out

Brighten up baby's first springtime with a walk through a world filled with cheerfully coloured flowers and animals.

 # Butterfly blanket

Techniques required

Hand appliqué, patchwork, quilting, hand or machine assembly

Size

91 x 91cm (36 x 36in)

Materials required

- Fabric for the patchwork pieces: 110 x 90cm (43½ x 35½in)
- Fabric for the lining: 91 x 91cm (36 x 36in)
- Assorted fabrics for the appliqué pieces, strips and border
- Polyester wadding: 150 x 100cm (60 x 40in)
- Rocaille beads
- Sewing thread in colours to match your fabrics
- Embroidery cotton

1 Prepare your materials.

Cut a 91 x 91cm square from your wadding and set it aside for step 5. Cut out the templates (pages 130–131). Transfer the pieces on to the appropriate fabrics, making the number of copies indicated. Cut the pieces out, adding a 5mm (¼in) seam allowance around each one. Clip notches in the seam allowances and fold them on to the reverse, wrong sides together. Cut out the same pieces in your remaining wadding, without adding seam allowances this time. For the patchwork, mark out one 40 x 40cm (15¾ x 15¾in) square and twelve 20 x 20cm (7 ⅞ x 7 ⅞in) squares, adding a 1cm (³/₈in) seam allowance around each one. Cut the squares out. Mark out the following strips, adding a 1cm (³/₈in) seam allowance around each one: two 4.5 x 40cm (1¾ x 15¾in) strips and two 4.5 x 49cm (1¾ x 19¼in) strips for the centre panel frame; twelve 3 x 20cm (1¼ x 7 ⅞in) strips to divide the small squares, and two 4 x 89cm (1½ x 35in) strips and two 4 x 91cm (1½ x 35 ⅞in) strips for the border. Cut them out.

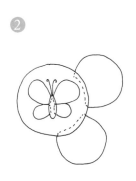

2 Centre panel.
Appliqué butterfly no.1 to the centre of flower no.1, backing each piece with wadding. Embroider the antennae and sew on two beads for the eyes. Place wadding under the centre of the flower, then appliqué the centre of the flower to the centre of the largest square, on top of your petals backed with wadding. Appliqué the petals. Sew the two smaller strips of the frame to the sides of the square 1cm (³/₈in) from the edges, right sides together, then sew the two other strips to the top and bottom.

3 Squares.

Appliqué a flower or butterfly to the centre of each square, backing each piece with wadding. For the butterflies, embroider antennae and sew on beads for the eyes.

4 Patchwork.

Work right sides together, 1cm (³⁄₈in) from the edges of your fabric. Make up two rows of four squares, separated by three strips. Make up two rows of two squares with one strip at each end and one in the centre. Sew the two small rows to the top and bottom of the centre panel, then sew the two large rows to the sides.

5 Quilting.

Lay your lining out face down. Place the wadding that you set aside in step 1 on top, followed by your patchwork, right side up. Pin to secure, then tack your work in a star shape to hold all the layers in place. Starting with the centre panel and working towards the edges, go around each motif in a running stitch. Sew around the centre flower three times and the other motifs twice, spacing your rows by 5mm (¼in).

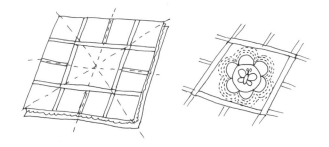

6 Border.

Add the border strips in the same way as you would add bias binding. Sew them to the patchwork 1cm (³⁄₈in) from the edges, and then to the lining with a slipstitch. Add the smaller strips to either side first, and then add the two remaining strips, folding the excess on to the inside at each end.

Tips

• The templates in this book are provided as a guide. Give free rein to your imagination and vary the sizes and shapes of the motifs or the design of the antennae.

• Appliqué small rounds of fabric to the butterfly wings to make the 'eyes'.

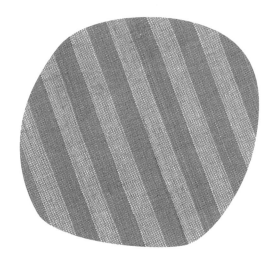

 # Customized t-shirts

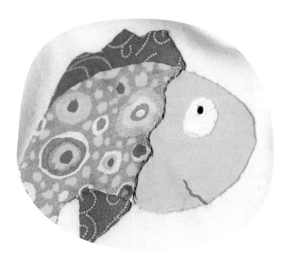

1 Prepare your materials.
Cut out the templates for your chosen model (page 126). For the butterfly t-shirt, prepare a template of heart no.1 (page 112). Transfer the pieces on to the appropriate fabrics and cut them out, adding a 5mm (¼in) seam allowance around each one. Clip notches in the seam allowances and fold them on to the reverse, wrong sides together.

2 Appliqué.
For the butterfly, transfer the heart on to the t-shirt using the template as a guide, then embroider it with a threaded running stitch. Appliqué the butterfly to the centre: add the wings first, then the body. Embroider the antennae in a flat stitch or a stem stitch. For the fish, appliqué the body to the head and fins. Go over the join between the head and the body in a stem stitch. Appliqué the eye. Embroider the pupil in a French knot and the mouth in a stem stitch. Appliqué the fish to the t-shirt.

Tips
• Add effect to your threaded running stitch by using a thicker thread for the threaded stitches under your running stitch. Why not combine three strands of stranded cotton with perle cotton?
• If you cut the fish eye from felt, do not add a seam allowance.
• Place a magazine inside the t-shirt to prevent you from sewing on to the back.
• Don't forget to add a personalized label to sign off your design! Embroider a label if you have time, or have one made at a haberdashery.

Travel bag

 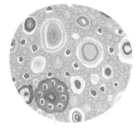   

Techniques required
Hand appliqué, hand or machine assembly

Size
25cm (10in) (width) x 12cm (4¾in) (depth) x 43cm (17in) (height)

Materials required
- Fabrics for the outer section: two 40 x 45cm (15¾ x 17¾in) lengths
- Fabric for the lining: 80 x 45cm (31½ x 17¾in)
- Fabric for the pocket: 14 x 20cm (5½ x 8in)
- Assorted offcuts of fabrics for the appliqué pieces (including a flesh-coloured fabric)
- Polyester wadding: 90 x 45cm (35½ x 17¾in)
- Braid: 14cm (5½in)
- Sewing thread in colours to match your fabrics
- Embroidery cotton

1 Prepare your materials.
The half-bag template is provided on page 136. Enlarge it to 200% and cut it out. Transfer it on to one of the pieces of fabric for the outer section, then transfer it on to the other piece, turning it over to give you a mirror image. Transfer it on to the lining fabric, making two mirror-image copies, and make two copies in your wadding. Cut out these six pieces, adding a 1cm (³⁄₈in) seam allowance around each one. To line the pocket, mark out a 12 x 18cm (4¾ x 7in) rectangle and cut it out, adding a 1cm (³⁄₈in) seam allowance around the outside. Cut out the templates for the appliqué pieces (page 137). Transfer the pieces on to the appropriate fabrics. Cut them out, adding a 5mm (¼in) seam allowance around each one. Clip notches in the seam allowances and, except for the bibs, fold them on to the reverse, wrong sides together. Cut out the heads of the bear and baby, the bottle and the bottle teat from your wadding, without adding a seam allowance.

2 Bag: appliqué.
Embroider the eyes on the baby's head in a French knot and embroider the mouth in a stem stitch. Add a small horizontal stitch for the nose. Place the two bibs one on top of the other, right sides together, and sew 5mm (¼in) from the edge, leaving the straight edge open. Turn your work out. Go around the outline in a running stitch. Embroider the mouth on the bear's muzzle, then appliqué the muzzle to the head and embroider the eyes on the head in a French knot. Appliqué the baby and the bear to the outer fabric as shown in the template: add the body first, followed by the head backed with wadding. Insert the top of the bib under the baby's head and the base of the ears under the bear's head. Leave the rest of the bib hanging free. Embroider the baby's arms with the hand on the body of the bear, and then the tuft of hair. Embroider the bear's arms.

3 Pocket.

Embroider the markings on the bottle. Appliqué the bottle to the centre of the pocket, backing the bottle and teat with wadding. Appliqué the braid at the top, at least 1.5cm (⁵⁄₈in) from the top edge. Position the pocket on the pocket lining, right sides together. Sew along the top 1cm (³⁄₈in) from the edge. Turn your work out. Pin the pocket to the outer fabric with the appliqué pieces, right sides together, in the corner shown in red on the template. Sew the side 1cm (³⁄₈in) from the edge. Flip the pocket on to the right side.

4 Assembly.

Place the two outer sections of the bag one on top of the other, right sides together, with the pocket inside. Sew the sides and the two bottom sections together with a seam 1cm (³⁄₈in) from the edges, then sew the side pieces to the base, ensuring that you include the bottom of the pocket in your stitching. Sew the top of the handle together. Turn the bag out. Fold the top edge over by 1cm (³⁄₈in), wrong sides together. Tack the lining pieces to your wadding pieces, right side up, then sew them together in the same way as for the outer section of the bag, but without the pocket this time. Trim the wadding close to the seams and trim to 1cm (³⁄₈in) from the edge of the fabric on the openings and the handle. Fold the seam allowance over on to the wadding. Place inside the bag. Sew the top edges together with an embroidered running stitch.

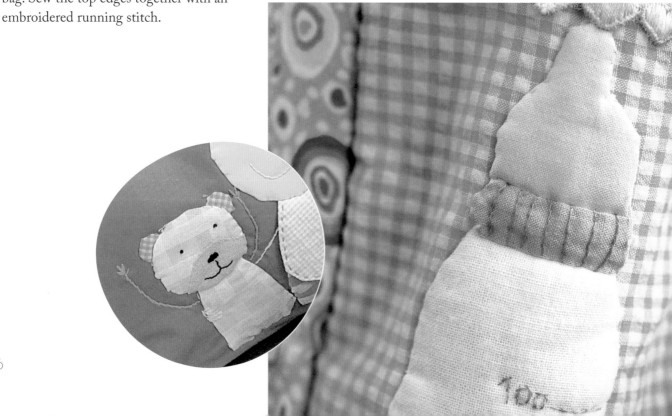

 # Springtime sunhat

Technique required
Hand appliqué

Materials required
• 1 sunhat
• Assorted offcuts of fabric
• Embroidery cotton

Tip
Vary the shape of your butterfly wings to add a creative touch to your sunhat.

1 Prepare your materials.
Cut out the templates (page 116). Transfer the pieces on to the appropriate fabrics, making the number of copies indicated. Cut them out, adding a 5mm (¼in) seam allowance around each one. Clip notches in the seam allowances and fold them on to the reverse, wrong sides together.

2 Appliqué.
Appliqué the flower to the top of the hat. Add the petals first, then the centre of the flower. Appliqué one butterfly on each side, overlapping the wings slightly. Embroider the antennae in a stem stitch and the swirls in a running stitch.

A world of discovery

Customizable, soft, unbreakable, easy to carry and washable – these fabric toys are stuffed with quality.

 Book of animals

Techniques required
Hand appliqué, patchwork, hand or machine assembly

Size
14.5 x 14.5cm (5¾ x 5¾in) (closed)

Materials required
- White fabric: 70 x 35cm (27½ x 13¾in)
- Offcuts of plain fabric for the characters
- Offcuts of felt for the features (inner ears, cheeks, spots, eyes, etc.)
- Fabrics for the cover patchwork: 9 different offcuts
- Fabrics for the strips on the pages: 30 different offcuts divided into six colourways
- Polyester wadding: 65 x 30cm (25½ x 12in)
- Ribbon: 20cm (8in)
- 1 novelty bell
- Sewing thread in colours to match your fabrics
- Embroidery cotton

1 Prepare your materials.
Cut two 30 x 16.5cm (11 ⅞ x 6½in) rectangles from your wadding and set them aside for step 5. Cut out the templates (page 128). Transfer the pieces on to the appropriate fabrics and cut them out, adding a 5mm (¼in) seam allowance around the pieces that are not in felt. Clip notches in the seam allowances and fold them on to the reverse, wrong sides together. Cut out the heads of the animals in your remaining wadding, without adding a seam allowance.

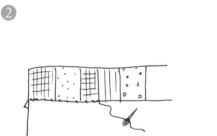

2 Strips. Cut thirty pieces 6cm (2 ³/₈in) wide and of varying lengths (at least 4cm/1½in) from your fabric for the strips on the pages. Sew them together end to end to make three strips 31cm (12¼in) in length, each comprising five pieces in one colourway and five pieces in another colourway. To do this, fold the inside edge of each piece over by 5mm (¼in), wrong sides together, place it on the outside edge of the next piece and appliqué.

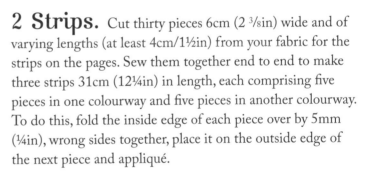

3 Pages. Cut four 31 x 12.5cm (12¼ x 5in) rectangles from your white fabric (including a 1cm/³/₈in seam allowance around each one). On one of the rectangles, fold the top edge (one of the lengths) over by 1cm (³/₈in), wrong sides together. Appliqué it to one of the strips so that it overlaps by 1cm (³/₈in). You should now have a double page measuring 31 x 16.5cm (12¼ x 6½in). Embroider a row of cross stitch at the top of your white fabric. Make up two more double pages in the same way.

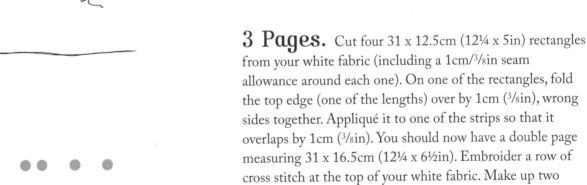

4 Appliqué. For each animal, appliqué the small pieces on to the large pieces: add the inner ears to the ears, the beak or muzzle to the head, and so on. Embroider the details. Appliqué one animal to the centre of each page you prepared in step 3, backing the head with wadding.

5 Cover. Cut out nine pieces to the sizes on page 127, adding a 1cm (³⁄₈in) seam allowance around each piece (cut square A from an offcut of white fabric). Appliqué the baby's face on to square A. Appliqué the cheeks, then add the features in your embroidery thread. Working 1cm (³⁄₈in) from the edges, right sides together, assemble the patchwork in the following order. Sew piece B to the top of square A, one piece C to the right-hand edge and the other piece C to the bottom edge, then sew one piece D to the left-hand edge. You should now have an 11.5 x 11.5cm (4½ x 4½in) square. Sew the other piece D to the top, one piece E to the right-hand edge and the other piece E to the bottom edge, then sew piece F to the left-hand edge. You should now have a 16.5 x 16.5cm (6½ x 6½in) square. Fold the left-hand edge over by 1cm (³⁄₈in), wrong sides together.

Cut out one heart no.4 (page 112) from your last piece of fabric, adding a 5mm (¼in) seam allowance all round. Clip notches in the seam allowance and fold it back, wrong sides together. Lay the patchwork on your remaining white rectangle, lining it up on the right, and appliqué the folded edge. Appliqué the heart in the centre of the left-hand page (the back of the cover).

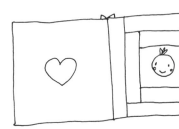

6 Assembly.

Assemble the three double pages end to end, right sides together, by sewing 1cm (³⁄₈in) from the edges of the short ends. Lay your work out right side up. Fold the double page on the left over the double page in the centre, right sides together, and place one of the rectangles of wadding set aside in step 1 on top, lining it up with the seam. Sew the top and bottom of pages 2–3 1cm (³⁄₈in) from the edges. Clip notches at the corners, trim the wadding close to the stitching, then turn out. Fold the double page on the right over the double page in the centre, right sides together, and place your last

rectangle of wadding on top, lining it up with your stitching. Sew the top and bottom of pages 4–5 1cm (³⁄₈in) from the edges. Clip notches at the corners, trim the wadding close to the stitching, then turn your work out.

Place the cover at the back of the pages, right side against the wadding, and with the patchwork section behind page 1. Sew the three sides of page 1 1cm (³⁄₈in) from the edges. Clip notches at the corners, trim the wadding close to the stitching and turn your work out. On the back cover and page 6, fold the seam allowances back by 1cm (³⁄₈in), wrong sides together. Trim the wadding close to the seam allowances. Thread the end of the ribbon into your work at the centre, then sew the edges together with a slipstitch. Attach the bell to the ribbon.

My garage

Techniques required

Hand appliqué, hand assembly

Size

10.5cm (4 ¹⁄₈ in) (width) x 14.5cm (5¾in) (depth) x 17cm (6¾in) (height)

Materials required

- Fabric for the exterior walls and floor: 70 x 20cm (27½ x 8in)
- Fabric for the roof exterior: 35 x 15cm (13¾ x 6in)
- Fabric for the interior: 60 x 25cm (24 x 10in)
- Assorted offcuts of fabric for the appliqué pieces
- Polyester wadding: 60 x 25cm (24 x 10in)
- Acetate film: 60 x 25cm (24 x 10in)
- Ric-rac braid: 105cm (41½in)
- 7 buttons: 4 for the vehicles,
  1 star-shaped button for the fuel pump,
  2 for the clasp
- Fine cord: 30cm (12in)
- Sewing thread in colours to match your fabrics
- Embroidery cotton

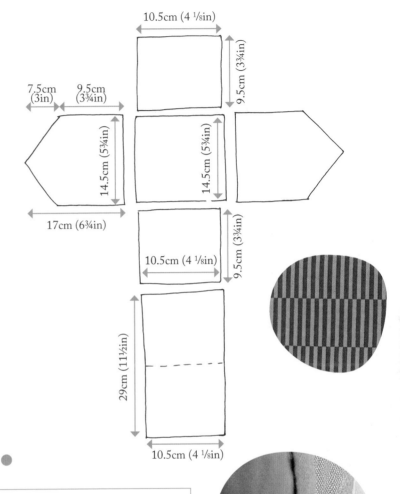

	Finished size	Exterior fabric	Interior fabric	Wadding	Acetate
Floor	10.5 x 14.5cm (4 ¹⁄₈ x 5¾in)	1 x	1 x	1 x	1 x
Side gables	see diagram	2 x	2 x	2 x	2 x
Front and rear walls	10.5 x 9.5cm (4 ¹⁄₈ x 3¾in)	2 x	2 x	2 x	2 x
Roof	14.5 x 10.5cm (5¾ x 4 ¹⁄₈in)	2 x		2 x	2 x
	29 x 10.5cm (11½ x 4 ¹⁄₈in)		1 x		

1 Prepare the panels.

Mark out the pieces indicated in the table above. Cut them out from the appropriate fabrics, adding a 5mm (¼in) seam allowance around each one. Do not add a seam allowance to your wadding and acetate pieces.

2 Prepare your appliqué pieces.

Cut out the templates (page 115). Transfer them on to the appropriate fabrics and cut them out, adding a 5mm (¼in) seam allowance around each one. Clip notches in the seam allowances, then fold them on to the reverse, wrong sides together.

3 Appliqué. Decorate the panels of the garage as follows.

Rear wall: exterior. Appliqué the breakdown truck. Outline the window and the bodywork in a stem stitch, then embroider the door and the winch. Sew on two buttons for the wheels.

Right gable: exterior. Appliqué the car. Outline the windows and bodywork in a stem stitch. Sew on two buttons for the wheels. Appliqué the fuel pump. Embroider the details. To make the hose, sew a long loose stitch in thick cotton and secure at the top with small stitches in a thinner black cotton. Sew the star-shaped button to the tank.

4 Making the garage. Using the diagram of the doll's house on page 24 as a guide, make up each panel of the garage as follows. Lay the interior fabric out face down. Place the acetate and then the wadding on top. Fold the seam allowances on the fabric over the wadding. Place the exterior fabric on top of your work, right side up, with the folded seam allowance on top of the seam allowance of the interior fabric. Sew the two pieces of fabric together with a slipstitch. To make the roof, make up the two sides, then sew them to the interior roof fabric, inserting the ends of the cord between them. Appliqué your ric-rac braid around the roof.

5 Assembly. Use a slipstitch and work with a length of doubled-up thread. Sew the side gables to either side of the floor, on the long edges. Sew the front wall to one of the short sides and then the rear wall to the other. Sew the side gables to the rear wall. Sew one side of the roof to the main section, at the back of the garage.

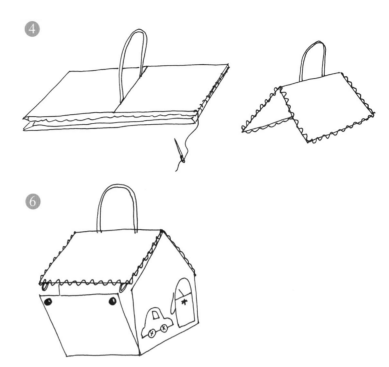

6 Clasp. Sew the buttons for the clasp on either side of the exterior front wall, approximately 5mm from the top edge. Embroider two straps under the roof opposite the buttons.

Tips

• Before adding the appliqué pieces, ensure that the walls are the right way up. They should be 10.5cm (4 1/8in) across and 9.5cm (3¾in) high.

• If you are unable to get hold of acetate sheets, use plastic office folders instead.

• The padding and acetate can be replaced with stiff wadding, which you can purchase from haberdasheries and on the internet.

• Vary your fabrics from one panel to the next, using the sizing table as a guide. In the photographed model, for example, the floor is cut from a checkerboard fabric to add an authentic look.

• Appliqué another car with a slightly different shape to the left gable of the garage.

• Use the garage in conjunction with the doll's house, which is featured on pages 20–24.

Carry play mat

Techniques required
Hand and machine appliqué,
hand or machine assembly

Size
Diameter: 98cm (38½in)

Materials required
- Green fabric: 105 x 105cm (42 x 42in)
- Fabric for the outside of the bag: 105 x 105cm (42 x 42in)
- Blue fabric: 45 x 15cm (18 x 6in)
- Fabric for the road: 90 x 50cm (36 x 20in)
- Assorted offcuts of fabric for the appliqué pieces (you can use felt for the cars, the sheep and the doors of the houses)
- Offcut of felt for the bridge
- 4 buttons
- Bias binding: 3.25m (3½yd)
- Cord: 7m (7½yd)
- Sewing thread in colours to match your fabrics
- Perle cotton and stranded cotton in black

1 Prepare your materials.

Fold your green fabric into four and cut the open edges into curves to obtain a circle with a 50cm (19¾in) radius. Repeat with the fabric for the outside of the bag. To make the road, mark out sections 7cm (2¾in) wide to make a loop with twists and turns. Draw the pond on your blue fabric and two sections 5cm (2in) wide for the stream. Cut out the templates (pages 134–135) and transfer them on to the appropriate fabrics. Cut out all your pieces, adding a 5mm (¼in) seam allowance around each one. Do not add a seam allowance to your felt pieces. Clip notches in the seams and fold them on to the reverse, wrong sides together.

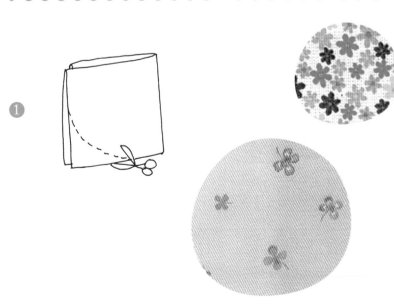

2 Appliqué.

Pin the sections of the road to the fabric end to end, overlapping them by 5mm (¼in) (to do this, fold the seam allowance over on one side). Appliqué them to the green fabric, sewing the long edges with a machine running stitch and the short edges by hand. Appliqué the pond and the stream on either side. Pin strips of felt side by side to make the bridge and appliqué them, embroidering rows of backstitch at the ends and adding French knots for nails. Appliqué the houses, adding the façades first and then the roofs. Embroider smoke in a stem stitch with perle cotton above houses with a chimney. Appliqué the trees, adding the trunks and then the foliage. Appliqué the field. Position the sheep on top and embroider the details using a strand of black stranded cotton. Appliqué the cars and sew on buttons for wheels. Use a strand of black stranded cotton to embroider the characters.

3 Assembly.

Cut your bias binding into two pieces of equal length. Unfold the pieces and tack them around your circle of green fabric, right sides together. Fold the ends back on themselves to obtain a good fit end to end. Place the circle of fabric for the outside on top, right sides together. Sew around the outside 1cm (⅜in) from the edge, leaving a gap of approximately 10cm (4in). Turn your work out. Sew up the gap with a slipstitch. Fold the bias binding back on itself by 1cm (⅜in), wrong sides together, flip this hem over the outer fabric and topstitch 5mm (¼in) from the edge. With the aid of a safety pin, thread your cord twice around the sleeve you have created: bring the two ends out at the same hole and tie them together. Bring a loop out at the other hole and tie a knot to secure.

Tips

• Cut the sections for the road and the stream from brown paper. Lay them out on your circle of green fabric to check that they fit together and you are happy with the layout. When you are satisfied, transfer the shapes on to the appropriate fabrics.

• Give free rein to your creativity and create a play mat that will appeal to the child who will receive it: add cars, flowers or animals, replace the houses with shops with embroidered signs, add junctions and dead ends – the possibilities are endless!

• Use felt for some of your appliqué details. Without a seam allowance you can adjust the size of the pieces while you decorate your fabric.

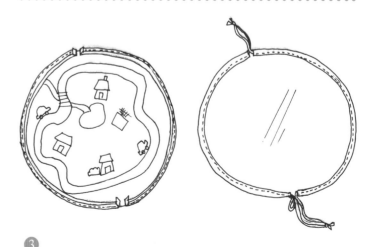

③

Activity wall hanging

Techniques required

Hand and machine appliqué,
hand or machine assembly

Size

55 x 39cm (21½ x 15½in)
(not including pennants)

Materials required

- Butter muslin: 55 x 32cm (21½ x 12½in)
- Blue fabric for the sky: 55 x 25cm (21½ x 10in)
- Green fabrics for the grass: 55 x 10cm (21½ x 4in)
  plain green; 4 different printed green offcuts
- Fabric for the centre panel: 55 x 12cm (21½ x 4¾in)

- Fabric for the lining: 55 x 40cm (21½ x 15¾in)
- For the appliqué pieces: assorted offcuts of fabric, felt, oilcloth, etc.
- Fabrics, felt and bells for the pennants (see box below)
- Wadding
- Buttons: 2 for the car wheels, 1 for the door of the house,
  1 for the cherry on the cake
- 2 bias bindings: 60cm (24in) and 80cm (32in)
- Length of ric-rac braid
- Lengths of ribbon
- Sewing thread in colours to match your fabrics
- Embroidery cotton
- Stranded cotton and perle cotton for the features of the characters

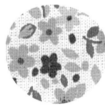

1 Prepare your materials.

Cut out the templates (pages 120–122) and
transfer them on to the appropriate fabrics
(mark out pieces 1 to 4 on your printed green
fabrics and cloud 6 on your wadding; mark out
the door of the house, the two copies of piece
26 and one of the copies of pieces 14 to 18 on
your felt). To make the grass on the bottom
panel, cut an undulating shape in one of the
long sides of your plain green fabric and cut a
small hill from one of your printed fabrics.
Cut the pieces out, adding a 5mm (¼in) seam
allowance around each one. Do not add a seam
allowance to your felt pieces and pieces that you
will appliqué with a zigzag stitch (see the tips
on page 81). Clip notches in the seam
allowances and fold them on to the reverse,
wrong sides together. Cut the body and head of
character no.7 and the foliage of trees 8 and 19
from your wadding. Cut the muslin and the
fabric for the sky in half lengthways.

Pennants

Dimensions for your felt triangles:
- five letters: 9.5 x 14cm (3¾ x 5½in)
- six letters: 8 x 12cm (3 1/8 x 4¾in)
- seven letters: 7 x 11.5cm (2¾ x 4½in)
- eight letters: 6.5 x 9cm (2½ x 3½in)

On your fabric, mark out pieces that are 6mm (¼in)
narrower and 6mm (¼in) shorter and add a 5mm (¼in)
seam allowance around each one.

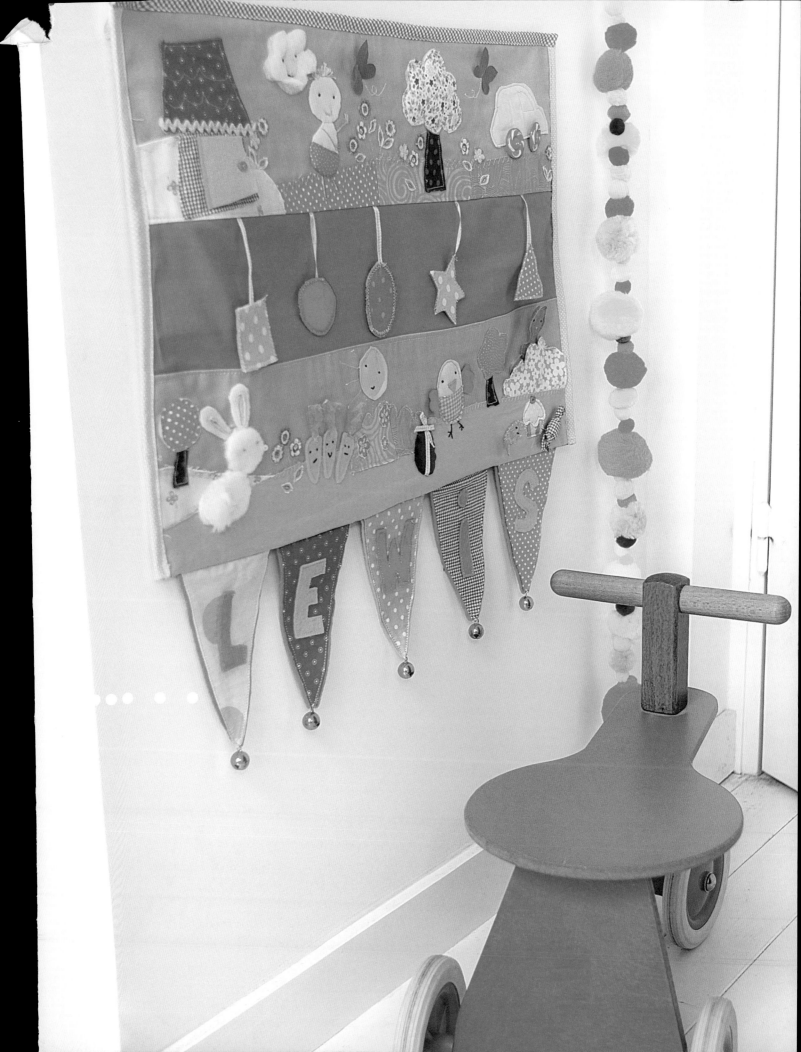

2 Top panel.

Work on one of your muslin strips. Except for the sky and the grass, leave a space of at least 1cm (³⁄₈in) around your pieces. Line up one strip of blue fabric with the top edge. Lay out pieces 1 to 4, opening out their seam allowances to line them up with the bottom edge and the sides of the muslin. Appliqué them by hand, sewing long stitches representing blades of grass or with a very short zigzag stitch. Appliqué the house in a machine running stitch: add the façade, then the roof, sewing on your ric-rac braid at the same time. Sew scalloped rows for the tiles. Sew the left edge of the door. Embroider the face to piece 29 and appliqué it behind the door. For character 7, embroider the face, sew the pants to the body and appliqué by hand, backing the pieces with wadding. Now embroider the arms, legs and the hair. Cut your butterflies from oilcloth. Do not appliqué the butterflies; attach them with an embroidered line to make the body. Attach the flowers by embroidering a large cross on the top. Appliqué the other items in a machine running stitch. Back the foliage of tree 8 with wadding. Embroider the details. Sew buttons to the door of the house and the car.

3 Bottom panel.

Place the sky and the two grass pieces on your remaining length of muslin in the same way as for the top panel. Unfold the seam allowance on the straight edges of two of your bush 22 pieces. Sew them together, wrong sides together.

Place them under the grass, lined up with the right-hand side of the panel. Appliqué the grass. Appliqué the bushes to the sky, leaving the top open to make a pocket.

Sew the heart to one cat 26, then embroider the nose and eyes. Place the two cats one on top of the other, thread the end of a ribbon between the two body pieces between the hind legs, and sew them together. Sew the other end of the ribbon behind the bush pocket. Appliqué the remaining bush with a machine running stitch (or split the bush into two pieces, cut them out from different fabrics and sew them together before appliquéing them). Leaving a gap of at least 1cm (³⁄₈in) around the pieces, appliqué rabbit 20, egg 23 and fish 27 by hand, attach the flowers in the same way as before, and appliqué the other pieces with a machine running stitch. Remember to back the foliage of tree 19 with wadding. To make the sweet, cut a 7.5 x 5cm (3 x 2in) strip, fold the edges over by 1cm (³⁄₈in) and sew with a running stitch. Bring the ends together to make a cylinder. Insert a little wadding into the centre, secure with a few stitches and tie like a sweet wrapper by winding a length of thread around each end. Embroider the details. Sew your remaining button on to the cake. Appliqué a ribbon tied in a bow to the egg.

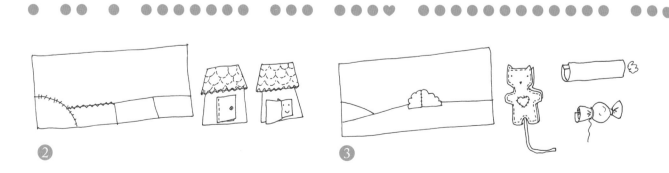

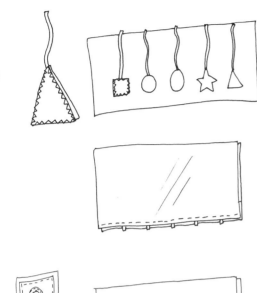

4 Centre panel. Place pieces 14 to 18 one on top of the other in pairs, wrong side of the fabric against the felt. Insert the end of a ribbon between the two layers. Sew around each piece in a zigzag stitch. Tack the other end of the ribbons to one of the long sides of the centre panel fabric, spacing them at regular intervals. Assemble the centre panel between the two other panels by sewing them together 1cm (³⁄₈in) from the edges, right sides together. Flatten out the seam allowances on the top and bottom panels and topstitch 3mm (¹⁄₈in) from the seams.

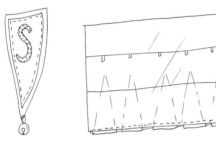

5 Pennants. Cut out the right number of triangles from your fabric (see box on page 78). Fold over the seam allowances, wrong sides together. Appliqué a hand-drawn felt letter to each triangle with a machine running stitch, then appliqué the triangle to a felt triangle. Sew a bell to the tip of each pennant.

6 Assembly. Line up the pennants along the bottom edge of your work, right sides together and with the points upwards, spacing them at regular intervals. Place the lining on top, right sides together. Sew 1cm (³⁄₈in) from the bottom edge. Turn your work out. Add your bias binding to each side and then to the top edge. To hang the wall hanging, sew two ribbon loops to the back of the panel in the corners.

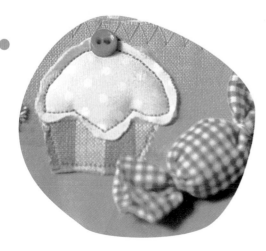

Tips

• When making this type of design it is not always necessary to fold back the edges of the pieces. Use non-fraying or low-fraying fabrics, cut them out without adding a seam allowance, and appliqué them by machine.

• To make your design appeal to baby's eyes and hands, use a variety of textures. In the photographed model the carrots are made from felt with fake fur stalks, the butterflies, sun and the Easter egg are made from oilcloth, and the rabbit is made from courtelle with a fake fur tail.

• If the child's name has more than eight letters, use a short word such as 'hello' or 'morning' instead.

Back to school

Make these two fantastic accessories to encourage children to keep their school supplies tidy.

Budding artist's pencil case

Techniques required
Hand appliqué, hand assembly

Size
14 x 20cm (5½ x 8in) (folded); 30 x 20cm (12 x 8in) (unfolded)

Materials required
• Outer fabric: 30 x 20cm (12 x 8in)
• Inner fabric: 30 x 20cm (12 x 8in)
• Fabrics for the pockets: 15 x 18.5cm (6 x 7¼in); 15 x 11.5cm (6 x 4½in)
• Assorted offcuts of fabric for the appliqué pieces
• Wadding: 30 x 20cm (12 x 8in)
• Bias binding: 105cm (41½in)
• Ric-rac braid: 45cm (18in)
• Ribbon: 15cm (6in) for the pocket, 20cm (8in) for the centre ribbon, 35cm (14in) for the tie
• Buttons: 4 small buttons for decoration, 1 large button for the tie
• Sewing thread in colours to match your fabrics
• Embroidery cotton

1 Prepare your materials. Cut out templates 1, 2 and 3 from page 129. Transfer the pieces on to the appropriate fabrics. Cut them out, adding a 5mm (¼in) seam allowance around each piece. Clip notches in the seam allowances and fold them on to the reverse, wrong sides together.

2 Appliqué. Mark out the area to be decorated on your outer fabric by pinning a row 2.5cm (1in) from the right-hand side and another 9cm (3½in) away from the first. Lay out your motifs, leaving a gap of at least 1cm (³⁄₈in) at the sides and the top, and a gap of at least 4cm (1½in) at the bottom. Appliqué the motifs, then embroider the details. Sew a length of ric-rac braid along your fabric at least 2cm (¾in) from the bottom edge. Sew the small buttons on top under the appliqué pieces.

3 Pockets.

On the larger of the two pockets, fold the top edge over widthways by 6cm (2 ³/₈in), wrong sides together, and press the fold with an iron. On the small pocket, fold the top edge over lengthways by 1cm (³/₈in) twice, wrong sides together, and appliqué the ribbon. Place the two pockets one on top of the other with the reverse of the small pocket on the right side of the large pocket, and line up the non-hemmed edges. Place the pockets on the inner fabric with the small pocket facing down, level with the bottom edge and 5.5cm (2 ¹/₈in) from the right-hand edge. Sew the pockets 1cm (³/₈in) from their left edge. Flip the large pocket on to the right side on the inner fabric. Sew vertical lines down the pocket. Flip the small pocket on to the right side over the large pocket. Place your remaining ric-rac braid on the left-hand side of the inner fabric at least 2cm (¾in) from the top edge.

Do not adjust the braid to fit the width of your fabric: this will allow you to insert a notebook or sheets of paper. Position the centre ribbon so that it sits on the join between the pockets and the inner fabric and secures the end of the ric-rac, and sew.

4 Assembly.

Pin the bias binding around your outer fabric, right sides together. Thread the end of your remaining ribbon into the centre on the side opposite your appliqué pieces. Sew the bias binding. Place the inner and outer fabrics one on top of the other, wrong sides together, with the wadding in between. Fold the bias binding over the inner fabric and sew with a slipstitch. Attach the button to the end of the ribbon.

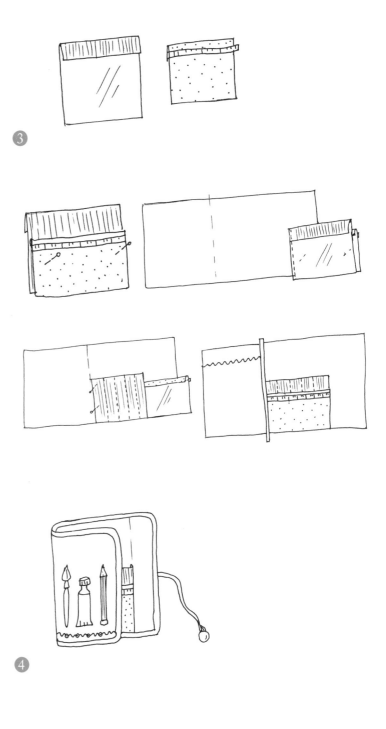

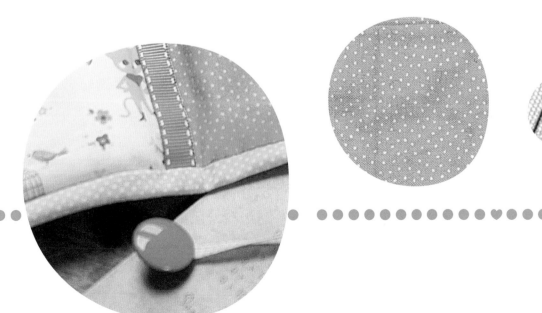

Sketch pouch

Techniques required
Hand appliqué, quilting, hand assembly

Size
28 x 22cm (11 x 8¾in) (folded);
58 x 22cm (22¾ x 8¾in) (unfolded)

Materials required
- Outer fabrics: 46 x 24cm (18 x 9½in); 16 x 24cm (6¼ x 9½in)
- Inner fabric: 60 x 24cm (24 x 9½in)
- Fabric for the pocket: 14 x 19cm (5½ x 7½in)
- Assorted offcuts of fabric for the appliqué pieces and the label
- Polyester wadding: 58 x 22cm (23 x 8¾in); 1 small offcut
- Ribbon: 48cm (19in)
- Cord: 15cm (6in)
- 1 button
- Sewing thread in colours to match your fabrics
- Stranded cotton
- Bristol board: 58 x 22cm (23 x 8¾in)
- Fabric spray adhesive

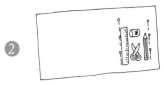

1 Prepare your materials.
Cut out templates 1, 4, 5, 6 and 7 from page 129. Transfer the pieces on to the appropriate fabrics. For the embroidered panel on the label, mark a 4 x 5cm (1½ x 2in) rectangle. Cut out all the pieces, adding a 5mm (¼in) seam allowance around each one. Clip notches in the seam allowances and fold them on to the reverse, wrong sides together. Cut out one eraser 5 from wadding, without seam allowance.

2 Appliqué. Mark out the area you will
decorate on your larger outer fabric piece by pinning a vertical row 3cm (1¼in) from the right-hand edge, and another row 13cm (5 ⅛in) from the first. Lay out your motifs, positioning ruler 4 against the second row of pins, and leaving a gap of at least 2cm (3/4in) at the top and bottom. Appliqué the motifs, backing eraser 5 with wadding, and then embroider the details.

3 Quilting. Attach the short outer fabric piece to
the left-hand edge of the long outer fabric piece, right sides together, sewing 1cm (³/₈in) from the edge. Fold the four edges over by 1cm (³/₈in), wrong sides together. Pin the wadding underneath your work, tucking it under the hems. Embroider around each appliqué piece in a running stitch. Sew the button midway up the shorter length of fabric, approximately 5cm (2in) from the edge.

4 Label.
Using one strand of stranded cotton, embroider person 8 to the rectangle for the label in a stem stitch. Appliqué the rectangle to the top half of piece 7. Fold piece 7 in half, right sides together, and sew the sides 5mm (¼in) from the edges (see diagram opposite). Turn your work out. Fold the edges of the pointed section 5mm (¼in) on to the inside, insert the end of the cord between the two sides and sew together with a slipstitch.

5 Inside.
Fold the top edge of the pocket over widthways by 4cm (1½in), wrong sides together, and press the fold with your iron. Fold the three other sides over by 1cm (³⁄₈in), wrong sides together. Appliqué the pocket to the right side of the inner fabric, 2cm (¾in) from the right-hand edge and at least 2cm (¾in) from the bottom edge. Cut your ribbon into two pieces of equal length. Pin these lengths vertically to the right side of your inner fabric. Place one length 17cm (6¾in) from the right-hand edge and the other 19cm (7½in) from the left-hand edge. Sew them at their ends.

6 Assembly.
Make two vertical grooves in your Bristol board, one 14cm (5½in) from the right edge, the other 16cm (6¼in) from the left edge. Glue the board to the back of your inner fabric (with the pocket on the 14cm/5½in flap) and fold the excess on to the reverse. Place your work on the outer section, with the board against the wadding. Insert the end of the cord between the two layers in the centre of the flap with the appliqué pieces. Sew the four sides together with a slipstitch.

Tips
• For a more solid and washable pouch, replace the Bristol board with three rectangles cut from plastic office folders. You could also substitute the wadding and board for stiff wadding, which you can purchase from haberdasheries and on the internet.
• Why not use the pouch as an album for your class photos?

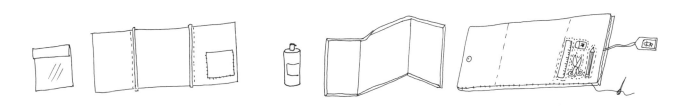

5   6

Tasty treats

Perfect for break-time snacks and birthday treats, children will love these mouth-watering appliqué designs.

Snack bag

Techniques required
Hand appliqué, reverse motifs,
hand or machine assembly

Size
24 x 26cm (9½ x 10¼in) (not including handle)

Materials required
- Fabric for the top of the front section: 30 x 20cm (12 x 8in)
- Fabric for the bottom of the front section and the back: 60 x 30cm (24 x 12in)
- Fabric for the handle: 10 x 30cm (4 x 12in)
- Lining: 60 x 30cm (20 x 12in)
- Assorted offcuts of fabric for the appliqué pieces
- Offcut of wadding
- Novelty buttons and standard two-holed buttons
- Rocaille beads
- 45cm (18in) zip fastener
- Sewing thread in colours to match your fabrics
- Embroidery cotton

1 Prepare your materials. The templates for the bag are provided on pages 138 and 139. Cut them out and transfer them on to the appropriate fabrics. You will need one top section piece, one bottom section piece, one complete fabric piece and two complete lining pieces. To make up a complete piece, place the two templates one above the other with the red markings together. Cut out all the pieces, adding a 1cm (³/₈in) seam allowance around each one. Cut out the templates for the appliqué pieces (page 139). Transfer the pieces on to the appropriate fabrics and cut them out, adding a 5mm (¼in) seam allowance around each one. Clip notches in the seam allowances and fold them on to the reverse, wrong sides together. Cut the biscuit and the cake cream from your wadding.

2 Decorative touches. Cut the centre out of the biscuit, clip notches in the edge and fold it back on to the reverse. Place a piece of red fabric underneath the biscuit and appliqué the edge of the circle to it. Embroider the outline of the biscuit in a blanket stitch. Appliqué the biscuit and the cake to the bottom section of the front of the bag, placing the wadding you cut out in step 1 underneath. To make the sweet, gather the fabric slightly on either side of the oval and appliqué, inserting a small piece of wadding underneath the fabric. Embroider rows of backstitch on the cake, then sew your beads to the cream. Embroider the characters on the top section of the front of the bag with a stem stitch (models are provided on page 138) and sew on your novelty buttons.

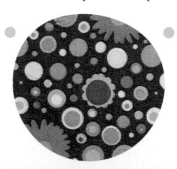

3 Handle. Fold the fabric in half lengthways, right sides together, and sew 1cm (³/₈in) from the edge. Turn your work out, place the seam in the centre of one side and iron.

4 Assembly. Working with right sides together, sew the two front sections together 1cm (³/₈in) from the edge. Place the front and back of the bag one on top of the other, right sides together. Sew around the bottom section 1cm (³/₈in) from the edge. Fold the edges of the opening over by 1cm (³/₈in), wrong sides together. On the reverse, pin one end of the handle to the centre of the top edge of the bag, and pin the other end on the opposite side on the front. Position the zip in the opening and embroider with running stitch.

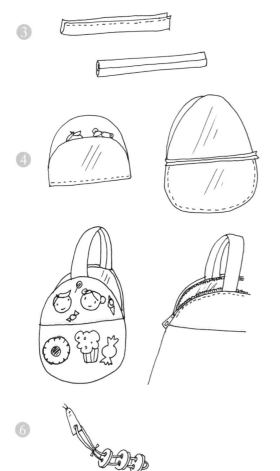

5 Lining. Place the two lining pieces one on top of the other, right sides together. Sew the base and sides 1cm (³/₈in) from the edge, to the same height as on the bag. Fold the edges of the opening over by 1cm (³/₈in), wrong sides together. Place the lining inside the bag, wrong sides together, and sew to the zip with a slipstitch.

6 Zip pull. Thread a length of thick embroidery cotton into one hole of your standard buttons, bring it out through the other holes in the opposite direction, thread it through the zip pull and tie the ends together.

Tips
• Replace the zip with velcro strips, which are quicker and easier to incorporate into your design.
• To decorate the zip pull, make a ball shape using buttons of increasing and then decreasing diameters.

 # Sweetie bag

Techniques required
Machine appliqué, hand or machine assembly

Size
18 x 17cm (7 x 6¾in) (not including handle)

Materials required
• Fabric for the main section: 40 x 20cm (15¾ x 8in)
• Fabric for the bottom of the front section: 20 x 10cm (8 x 4in)
• Fabric for the handle: 35 x 15cm (14 x 6in)
• Lining: 40 x 20cm (15¾ x 8in)
• Assorted offcuts of fabric for the appliqué pieces
• Wadding: 40 x 30cm (15¾ x 12in)
• Ric-rac braid: 20cm (8in)
• Braid: 65cm (25½in)
• Sewing thread in colours to match your fabrics

1 Prepare your materials.

The templates for the bag are provided on page 141. Cut them out and transfer them on to the appropriate fabrics. You will need two main section pieces, one bottom section (below the red markings) and two lining pieces. Mark out two 35 x 7cm (13¾ x 2¾in) strips for the handle and round off the corners at one end. Mark out two main section pieces and one handle on your wadding. Cut out all the pieces, adding a 1cm (³⁄₈in) seam allowance around each one. Cut out the templates for the appliqué pieces. Transfer them on to the appropriate fabrics. Mark out two 5 x 4cm (2 x 1½in) rectangles for the sweet on the handle. Cut out all the pieces without adding a seam allowance.

2 Appliqué. Pin the bottom section to one of the main sections. Sew your ric-rac braid so that it sits over the top edge. Appliqué the three sweets by machine in a very short zigzag stitch.

3 Assembly. Place the back and front sections one on top of the other, right sides together, and position them between the two main sections in wadding. Sew the base and sides 1cm (³⁄₈in) from the edges. Trim the wadding close to the seam. Turn the work out. Sew the two lining pieces together 1cm (³⁄₈in) from the edge, right sides together. Place the lining inside the bag, wrong side against the wadding. Fold the edges on to the outside and sew on the braid so it overlaps the two fabrics.

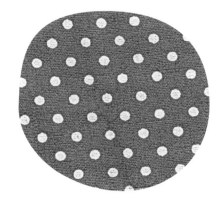

4 Handle.

Place the two handle pieces one on top of the other, right sides together, and place the wadding handle on top. Sew the sides and the rounded end 1cm (³⁄₈in) from the edges. Trim your wadding close to the seam. Turn your work out. Fold the edges of the opening 1cm (³⁄₈in) on to the inside and close with a slipstitch. Fold each of your sweet rectangles in half lengthways, right sides together. Sew the sides 5mm (¼in) from the edge. Turn your work out. Sew through both layers to gather the opening. Pin the circle of fabric to the rounded end of the handle, place the gathered edge of each rectangle underneath and appliqué with a zigzag stitch. Position the handle on the front of the bag as shown on the template, then sew to the folded part of the lining. Sew the other end to the back diagonally opposite, also on the lining.

Tip
If your appliqué fabrics are delicate or likely to fray, back them with iron-on fabric before cutting them out.

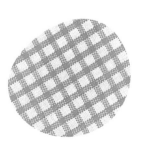

Baker's apron

Techniques required
Hand appliqué, hand assembly

Sizes
4/6 years [8/10 years]

Materials required
- Fabric for the main section: 60cm [70cm] x 70cm [80]cm (24in [27½in] x 27½in [31½in])
- Fabric for the pocket: 35 x 20cm (14 x 8in)
- Assorted offcuts of fabric for the appliqué pieces
- Ribbon: 35cm (14in) for the pocket; 10cm (4in) for the sweet; 10cm (4in) for the cake on the apron
- Ric-rac braid: 15cm (6in)
- Bias binding: 2.25m (2½yd)
- 2 buttons
- Small bugle beads
- Sewing thread in colours to match your fabrics

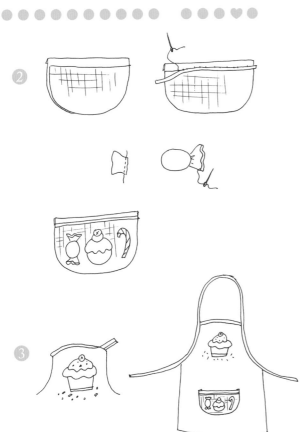

1 Prepare your materials.

The templates for the apron are provided on page 132. Enlarge them to 250%, then cut out your chosen size. The pocket is the same for both sizes. Transfer the two pieces on to your main fabric. Mark out a second pocket on the appropriate fabric, 2cm (¾in) shorter this time. Cut the pieces out, adding a 1cm (³⁄₈in) seam allowance around each one.

Cut out the templates for the appliqué pieces (page 133). Transfer the pieces on to the appropriate fabrics, then cut them out, adding a 5mm (¼in) seam allowance around each one. Clip notches in the seam allowances and fold them on to the reverse, wrong sides together.

2 Appliqué.
Fold the top edge of the pocket cut from your main fabric over by 5mm (¼in) twice, wrong sides together, and hem. Place the two pockets one on top of the other, lining them up along the sides and the base. Sew on your ribbon so that it overlaps the two pieces. Take the two layers of fabric and fold the non-hemmed edges over by 1cm (³⁄₈in), wrong sides together.

Appliqué pieces 2, 3 and 4 to the pocket. To make the sweet, gather the pieces of fabric slightly on either side of the oval and appliqué your short lengths of ribbon. Appliqué the ric-rac braid to the edge of the icing on the cake and sew a button on top. Appliqué cake 1 to the apron. Sew your ribbon around the base. Attach your remaining button to the top. Sew beads on the icing and around the cake.

3 Finishing touches.
Appliqué the pocket to the apron. Along the sides and the bottom of the apron, fold the fabric over by 5mm (¼in) twice, wrong sides together, and hem. Add bias binding along the top edge of the apron. Now add your remaining bias binding around the armholes, leaving a loop at the top for the neck and a tie on each side. Fold the bias binding over wrong sides together on the ties and loop and secure with a slipstitch.

In the springtime

"Mary, Mary, quite contrary
How does your garden grow?"
Two designs for green-fingered youngsters.

Gardener's apron

Techniques required

Hand appliqué, hand assembly

Sizes

4/6 years [8/10 years]

Materials required

- Fabric for the main section: 50cm [60cm] x 60cm [70]cm (20in [24in] x 24in [27½]in)
- Fabrics for the pocket: 35 x 15cm (14 x 6in); 35 x 10cm (14 x 4in)
- Assorted offcuts of fabric for the appliqué pieces
- Pompom braid: 25cm [35cm] (10in [14in])
- Bias binding: 220cm (86½in) for the apron; 45cm (18in) for the tulip stems
- Sewing thread in colours to match your fabrics
- Embroidery cotton

1 Prepare your materials.

The templates for the apron are provided on page 132. Enlarge them to 250%, then cut out your chosen size. The pocket is the same for both sizes. Transfer the three pieces on to the appropriate fabrics. Cut the pieces out, adding a 1cm (³⁄₈in) seam allowance around each one. Cut out the templates for the appliqué pieces (page 112). Transfer the pieces on to the appropriate fabrics, then cut them out, adding a 5mm (¼in) seam allowance around each one. Clip notches in the seam allowances and fold them on to the reverse, wrong sides together.

2 Appliqué.

Sew the two pocket fabrics together 1cm (³⁄₈in) from one of the long edges, right sides together. Fold the top edge over by 5mm (¼in) twice, wrong sides together, and hem. Fold the three other sides over by 1cm (³⁄₈in), wrong sides together. Appliqué the carrot, radish and peas. Embroider the details.

Sew the pocket to the apron. Cut the bias binding for the stems into three pieces, each a different length. Fold them in half, wrong sides together, place one end under the pocket and appliqué. Appliqué the tulips to the apron.

3 Finishing touches.

Fold the fabric along the sides and the bottom of the apron over by 5mm (¼in) twice, wrong sides together, and hem. Hem the top edge of the apron in the same way. Appliqué your braid to the top of the apron. Add the bias binding along the armholes, leaving a loop at the top for the neck and a tie on each side. Fold the bias binding over wrong sides together on the ties and loop and secure in place with a slipstitch.

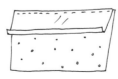
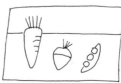

Tips
• To keep your peas round, gather the seam allowances around a card template (see page 9).
• Why not cut the apron from an old item of clothing, such as a man's shirt? Position your templates to make use of the hem at the bottom.

Egg-hunter's bag

Techniques required
Hand appliqué, hand or machine assembly

Size
16 x 20cm (6¼ x 8in) (not including handle)

Materials required
• Fabric for the main section: 18 x 48cm (7 x 19in)
• Lining: 18 x 48cm (7 x 19in)
• Assorted offcuts of fabric and felt for the appliqué pieces
• Ribbon 2.5cm (1in) wide: 65cm (25½in)
• Sewing thread in colours to match your fabrics

1 Prepare your materials.
Cut out the templates for the appliqué pieces (page 115). Transfer the pieces on to the appropriate fabrics (transfer the comb, eyes, beak and feet on to your felt). Cut the pieces out, adding a 5mm (¼in) seam allowance around the fabric pieces. Do not add a seam allowance to your felt pieces. Clip notches in the seam allowances.

2 Appliqué.
Sew together the three pieces that make up the body 5mm (¼in) from the edges, right sides together. Fold the edges of the resulting piece over by 5mm (¼in), wrong sides together. Appliqué the eyes, then embroider the eyelashes and the pupils. Appliqué the top edge of the beak with a running stitch. Place the wings one on top of the other in pairs, right sides together, and sew 5mm (¼in) from the edge, leaving the straight edge open. Turn your work out.

Fold the main fabric in half widthways, wrong sides together, and mark the fold. Pin your appliqué work to the front: place it in the centre, at least 7cm (2¾in) from the top edge and with the feet overlapping the fold a little. Unfold your fabric. Appliqué the hen: add the wings first, gathering them slightly, then the feet and the comb, and then the body.

3 Assembly.
Fold the main fabric in half, right sides together. Sew the sides 1cm (⅜in) from the edges. Fold the top edge over by 1cm (⅜in), wrong sides together. Turn your work out. Make up the lining in the same way and place it inside the bag, wrong sides together. Sew the top edges together with a slipstitch, then fold them on to the outside.

4 Handle.
To make the bow, cut a length of ribbon and sew the ends together to make a circle. Wrap a small piece of ribbon around the centre and secure with a couple of stitches on the reverse. Sew the bow to the centre of your remaining ribbon. Sewing through all the layers, secure the ends of the ribbon on either side of the bag so they sit on top of the seams on the flap.

Time for tea!

Bibs for babies and placemats for bigger kids: these easy-to-make designs will make every meal a fun one.

Mini placemats and napkin cases

Mini placemats

Techniques required
Hand appliqué, hand or machine assembly

Size
25 x 25cm (10 x 10in)

Materials required
FOR BOTH MODELS
• Background fabric: 25 x 25cm (10 x 10in)
• Assorted offcuts of fabric for the appliqué pieces
• Bias binding: 120cm (47¼in)
• Sewing thread in colours to match your fabrics
• Embroidery cotton
BLUE MODEL
• Bias binding for the straw: 15cm (6in)

1 Prepare your materials.
Cut out the templates for the appliqué pieces (pages 139 and 140). Transfer the pieces on to the appropriate fabrics. Transfer pieces 1 and 2 for the blue model and pieces 3 to 5 for the red model. Cut them out, adding a 5mm (¼in) seam allowance around each one. Clip notches in the seam allowances and fold them on to the reverse, wrong sides together.

2 Appliqué.
Pin the pieces to the background fabric and appliqué. For the blue model, fold the bias binding wrong sides together, sew with a slipstitch and place the end under the beaker. Embroider the details.

3 Finishing touches.
Add the bias binding around the outside of the background fabric. Make 45-degree angles at the corners. Sew with a slipstitch.

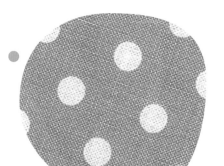

Tips
• To keep your cherries round, gather the seam allowances around a card template (see page 9).
• For a neater finish, place the background fabric on to a lining of the same size, wrong sides together, and add the bias binding, sewing through all the layers.
• Change the sizes of your fabrics to make larger or rectangular shaped placemats.
• Why not use the motifs from this model on other designs, such as a tablecloth for a doll?

Napkin cases

Techniques required
Hand appliqué, hand assembly

Size
21 x 12cm (8¼ x 4¾in)

Materials required
- Background fabric: 23 x 38cm (9 x 15in)
- Assorted offcuts of fabric for the appliqué pieces
- Sewing thread in colours to match your fabrics
- Embroidery cotton

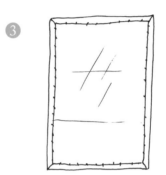

1 Prepare your

materials. Cut out the templates (page 144). Transfer the pieces on to the appropriate fabrics (reverse the cup if you wish). Cut the pieces out, adding a 5mm (¼in) seam allowance around each one. Clip notches in the seam allowances and fold them on to the reverse, wrong sides together.

2 Appliqué.
Lay your background fabric out widthways, right side up. Mark out the area that you will decorate by pinning a horizontal line 2cm (¾in) from the bottom edge, and another 10cm (4in) above the first. Leave a gap of at least 2cm (¾in) at the sides. Pin your pieces on and mark out the character to ensure that your layout is correct. Appliqué the pieces. Go around the lip of the cup and the inside of the spoon in a running stitch. Embroider the character: use a stem stitch for the face, a backstitch for the outline of the hair and a flat stitch for the hair itself.

3 Finishing touches.
Fold the four sides of the fabric over by 5mm (¼in) twice, wrong sides together, and hem. Fold the short end opposite your appliqué over by 12cm (4¾in), wrong sides together. Embroider the sides and the bottom edge in a blanket stitch, sewing through all the layers.

Colourful bibs

Technique required
Hand appliqué

Materials required
- 1 bib
- Assorted offcuts of fabric for the appliqué pieces (including a flesh-coloured fabric)
- Sewing thread in colours to match your fabrics
- Offcut of pink felt
- Embroidery cotton

Tip

For a smarter finish, make your own bib using a shop-bought model as a template. After adding the appliqué pieces, place the terry cloth on a lining of the same size, wrong sides together, and add bias binding around the outside, sewing through all the layers.

1 Prepare your materials. Cut out the templates for the appliqué pieces (pages 139 and 140). Transfer the pieces on to the appropriate fabrics. Transfer pieces 3, 6, 7, 8 and 9 for the blue model and pieces 6, 10, 11 and 12 for the pink model. Cut them out, adding a 5mm (¼in) seam allowance around each one. Clip notches in the seam allowances and fold them on to the reverse, wrong sides together. Cut two circles of felt for the children's cheeks, without adding a seam allowance this time.

2 Appliqué. Appliqué the mouth to the face, and then the cheeks, with a running stitch. Outline the mouth in a stem stitch. Embroider the eyes. Appliqué the face to the centre of the bib. To make the hair of the baby on the blue bib, embroider loops, securing each one with a small backstitch. To make the hair of the baby on the pink bib, embroider rows of French knots. Embroider the details on to the appliqué pieces and appliqué the pieces around the face.

Fabulous presents

It's often the smallest surprises that appeal to children most,
especially when presented in a fun way.

Advent calendar

Techniques required
Hand appliqué, hand or machine assembly

Size
80 x 80cm (31½ x 31½in)

Materials required
- Background fabrics: the photographed model uses 7 fabrics; you will need 30 x 30cm (12 x 12in) of each
- Fabric for the border: 85 x 60cm (33½ x 23½in)
- Lining: 72 x 72cm (28½ x 28½in)
- Fabric for the path: 70 x 40cm (27½ x 15¾in)
- Assorted offcuts of fabric for the appliqué pieces (including a flesh-coloured fabric)
- Muslin: 72 x 72cm (28½ x 28½in)
- Offcut of wadding
- Small sequins, rocaille beads, novelty buttons
- Sewing thread in colours to match your fabrics
- Embroidery cotton

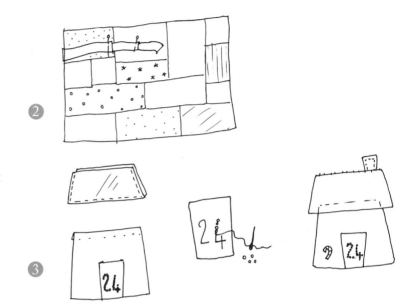

1 Prepare your materials.
Cut out the templates for the appliqué pieces (pages 142–143). Transfer the pieces on to the appropriate fabrics. Transfer two copies of the roof of the house, making the second copy a mirror image of the first. Transfer twenty-three presents in the three sizes to suit your taste. For the path, mark out sections 3cm (1¼in) wide, with four semi-circular sections for the turns (see Tip on page 108). Cut out all the pieces, adding a 5mm (¼in) seam allowance around each one. Clip notches in the seam allowances and, except for the roofs, fold the seam allowances on to the reverse, wrong sides together. Cut out the head of each child from wadding, without adding a seam allowance.

2 Background.
Cut squares and rectangles from the background fabrics to make up a piece of patchwork that covers your muslin, adding a 5mm (¼in) seam allowance around each piece. Fold the seam allowances on to the reverse. Appliqué the pieces by hand to the muslin.

3 Appliqué.
Pin the sections of the path to the background and appliqué them with a running stitch.

To make the two children, unfold the seam allowance on the head, appliqué the hair, then fold the seam allowance back on to the reverse. Embroider the mouth and eyes. Appliqué the children to the background fabric at the start of the path, backing the heads with wadding. Embroider the girl's pony tail.

Place the two roof pieces one on top of the other, right sides together. Sew the bottom edge and the sides 5mm (¼in) from the edges. Turn your work out. Fold the edges of the opening on to the inside by 5mm (¼in). Hem the top edge of the wall. Embroider the number 24 to the door in rocaille beads and appliqué it to the wall with a running stitch. Decorate the wall with buttons. Appliqué it to the background fabric at the end of the path, leaving the hemmed edge open. Pin the roof to the background fabric, placing the chimney underneath. Appliqué the top edge, sewing through all the layers to secure the opening.

4 Presents.
Hem the top edge of each present. Place a ribbon vertically down the centre, fold it on to the reverse at the bottom, leave about 10cm (4in) at the top and appliqué. Sew on the sequins. Pin the presents to the path, leaving space for the two Christmas trees. Appliqué them with a running stitch, leaving the hemmed side open. Sew a piece of ribbon on to the background fabric behind each present and tie it in a bow to the lower piece of ribbon. Sew novelty buttons on to the path between the presents.

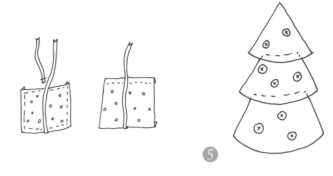

5 Christmas trees.
Decorate the Christmas tree pieces with small buttons. Pin them to the background fabric, starting from the base and overlapping the other sections.

6 Border.
Cut two 12 x 72cm (4¾ x 28 ³⁄₈in) strips and two 12 x 82cm (4¾ x 32¼in) strips. Fold the long sides over by 1cm (³⁄₈in), wrong sides together, then fold them on top of each other. Iron, then unfold. Place the background fabric and the lining one on top of the other, wrong sides together. Pin the smaller strips to either side of the background, right sides together, and sew 1cm (³⁄₈in) from the edges. Flip them over the lining, fold them over by 1cm (³⁄₈in), wrong sides together, and sew with a slipstitch. On the remaining strips, fold the ends over by 1cm (³⁄₈in), wrong sides together. Sew the strips to your work in the same way as before, then secure the ends with a slipstitch. Cut an 80 x 12cm (31½ x 4¾in) strip. Fold it in half lengthways, right sides together. Make 45-degree angles at the ends. Sew 1cm (³⁄₈in) from the edge, leaving an opening in the centre of the long side. Turn your work out and close the hole with a slipstitch. Tie the strip into a bow and sew to the top border in the centre.

Tip
Mark out your path on a large piece of brown paper and check that it fits when you have put together your background, taking into account the height of the presents and the house. Cut the paper into sections and transfer them on to your fabric.

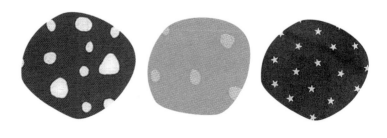

Surprise purses

Technique
Hand appliqué, hand or machine assembly

Size
8 x 11cm (3 ⅛ x 4 ⅜ in)

Materials required
- Fabric for the main section: 10 x 26cm (4 x 10¼in)
- Offcut(s) of fabric(s) or felt for the appliqué piece
- Sewing thread in (a) colour(s) to match your fabric(s)
- Soft tapestry cotton
- 2 beads, 1 button

DEPENDING ON THE MODEL
- Ribbon, beads, embroidery cotton, wadding

1 Prepare your materials.
Cut out the template for your chosen appliqué piece (page 117 for the mouse, page 112 for heart no.3, page 138 for the sweet; for the presents, mark out a square or rectangle to your required size). Transfer the pieces on to the appropriate fabric(s) and cut them out, adding a 5mm (¼in) seam allowance around each one, except for the felt pieces. Clip notches in the seam allowance(s) and fold on to the reverse, wrong sides together.

2 Appliqué. Fold your main fabric in
half widthways, wrong sides together. Pin your appliqué piece to the front, leaving a gap of at least 1cm (⅜in) at the sides and at least 4cm (1½in) at the top. Unfold your fabric.
Mouse. Appliqué the stomach to the body and the two pieces for each ear one on top of the other. Embroider the eyes with a French knot. Embroider a curved stitch for the mouth. Sew on a rocaille bead for the belly button.

Tips
- Cut your appliqué pieces from felt. This means you can work without a seam allowance and allows you to add extra relief to your motif.
- Take a look through the templates at the end of the book for other small motifs to appliqué to your surprise purses.

Appliqué the mouse: add the body first, then the head, inserting the base of the ears underneath. Embroider the tail, legs and whiskers, then sew on a bead for the end of the nose.
Heart. Appliqué the heart with a blanket stitch.
Sweet. Gather the fabric slightly on either side of the oval. Place a piece of wadding behind the oval and appliqué.
Presents. Place a vertical ribbon in the centre of the piece, fold the ends on to the reverse and sew. Appliqué the piece to the main fabric. Tie a ribbon in a bow and sew to the top of the present.

3 Finishing touches. Fold your fabric in
half, right sides together. Sew the sides 1cm (⅜in) from the edges. Fold the top edge over by 1cm (⅜in) twice, wrong sides together, and hem. Turn your work out. Thread a needle with soft tapestry cotton and sew around the bag under the hem in a long running stitch. Bring the ends of the cotton out on either side of one of the seams. Thread each of the ends into one hole of the button and then into a bead, and tie a knot in the end.

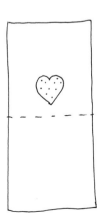

②

Templates

- - - - continuation of piece

— — markings

— embroidery, bead, button

Hearts

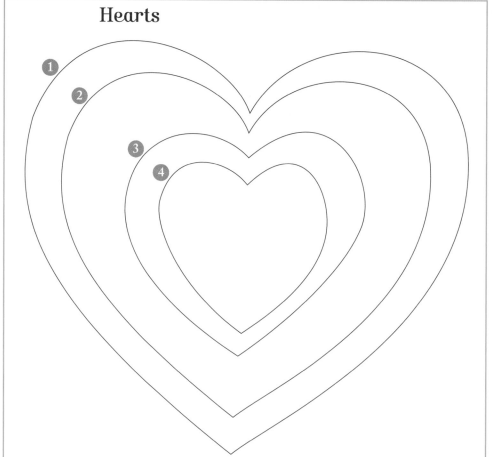

Gardener's apron
(pages 96–97)

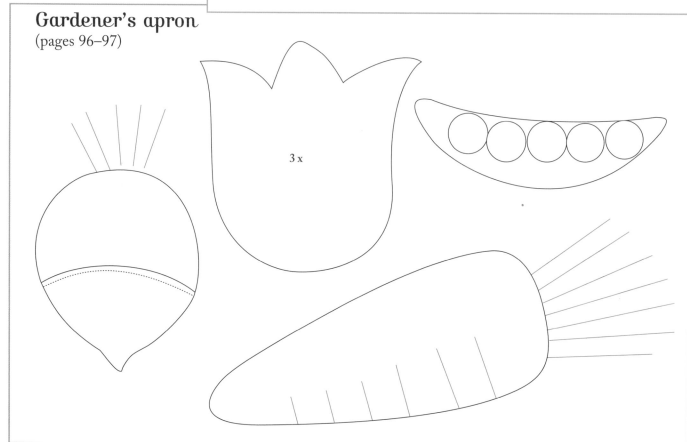

3 x

Blanket bag (pages 55–57)

Large pig

2 x

2 x

Small pig

2 x

2 x

2 x

2 x

2 x

Pretty in pink sports bags (pages 18–19)

Enlarge these templates to 125%.

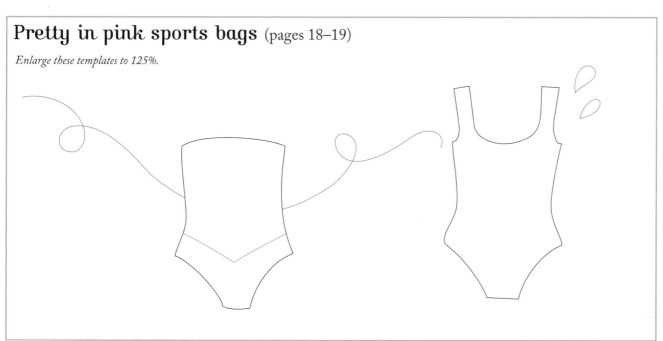

My doll's house (pages 20–25)

Enlarge these templates to 125%.

2 x

Occupants

2 x

2 x

2 x

2 x

Egg-hunter's bag
(pages 98–99)

2 x

2 x

My garage (pages 72–74)

Enlarge these templates to 125%.

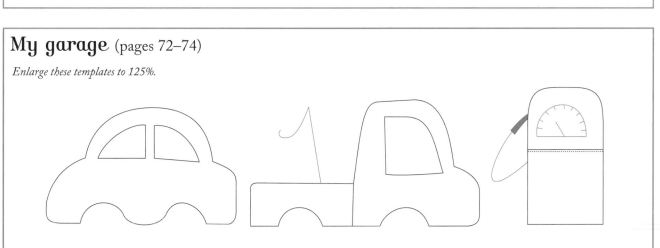

Springtime sunhat (page 67)

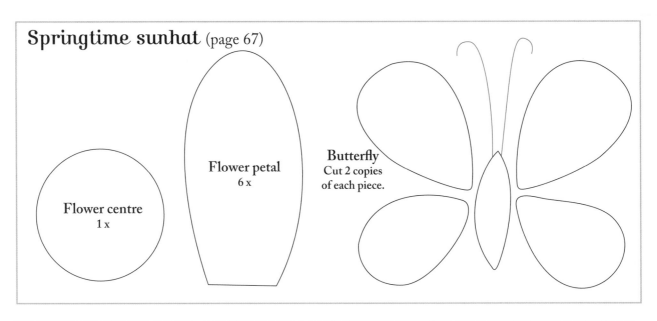

Flower centre
1 x

Flower petal
6 x

Butterfly
Cut 2 copies
of each piece.

Quilted cushion-blanket (pages 50–51)

My favourite cushion
(pages 14–17)

Surprise purses
(pages 110–111)

Legs

Baby's first bag
(pages 44–45)

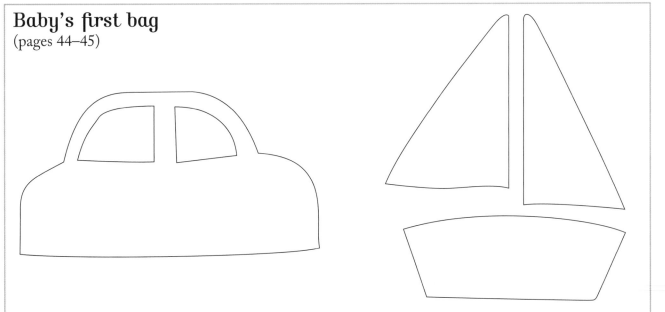

Pyjama case (pages 28–33)

Enlarge these templates to 200%.

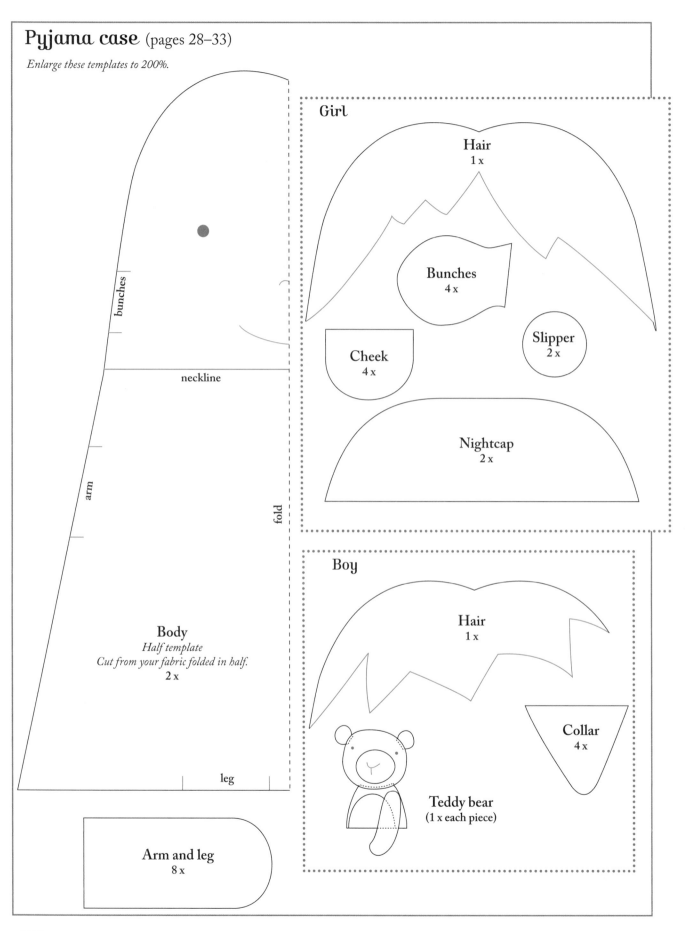

Girl

Hair
1 x

Bunches
4 x

Slipper
2 x

Cheek
4 x

Nightcap
2 x

bunches

neckline

fold

arm

Body
Half template
Cut from your fabric folded in half.
2 x

leg

Arm and leg
8 x

Boy

Hair
1 x

Collar
4 x

Teddy bear
(1 x each piece)

Toy tidy
(pages 42–43)

Enlarge these templates to 125%.

Activity wall hanging (pages 78–81)

Enlarge these templates to 125%.

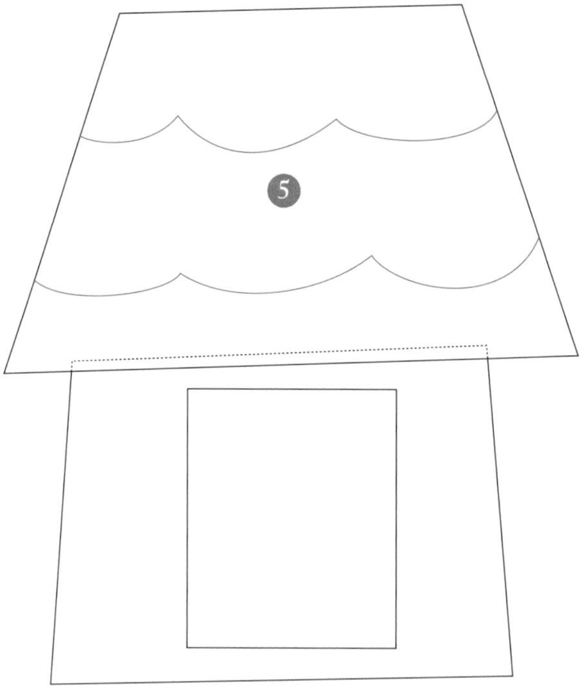

5

8

6

13

12 several copies,
some mirror image

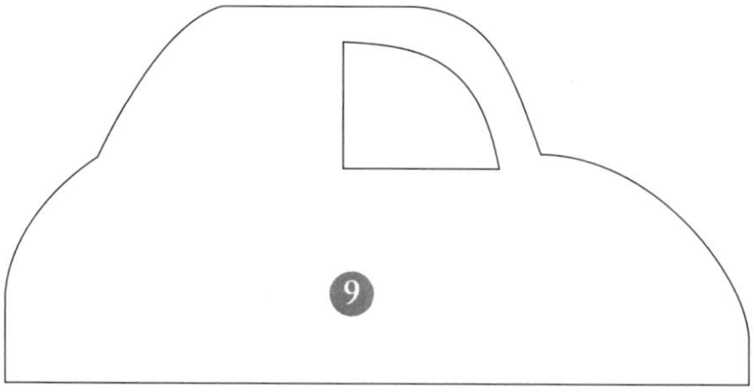

29

7

9

16 2 x

18 2 x

17 2 x

14 2 x

15 3 x

19

25

11 1 x + 1 x mirror image

20

24

21 3 x 3 x

26

27

23

28

22 2 x + 1 x mirror image

2 x

Activity wall hanging (pages 78–81)

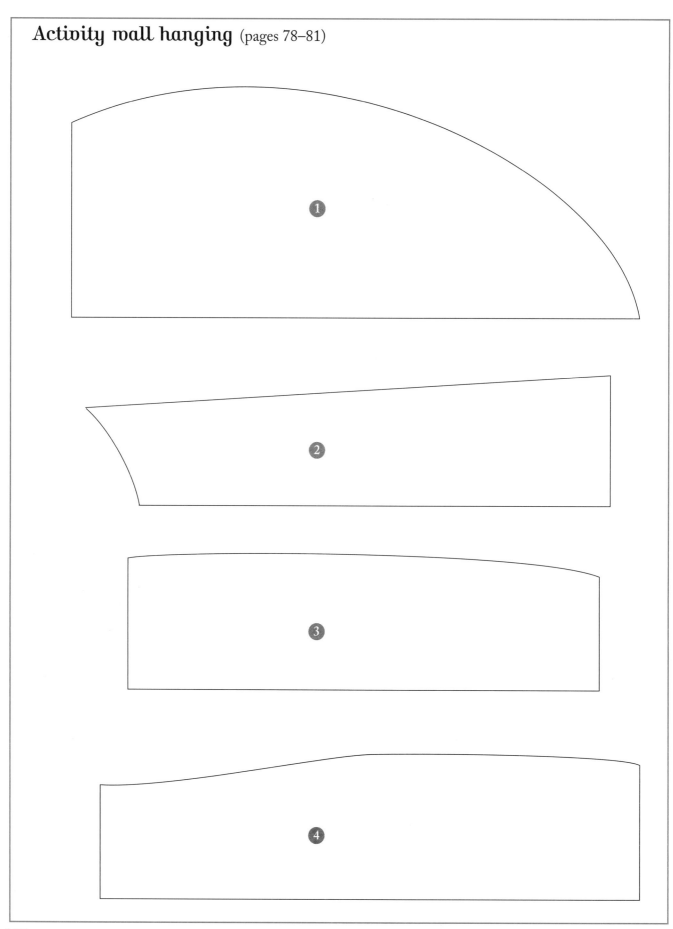

Bonnet and bootee set

(pages 46–49)

Enlarge these templates to 125%.

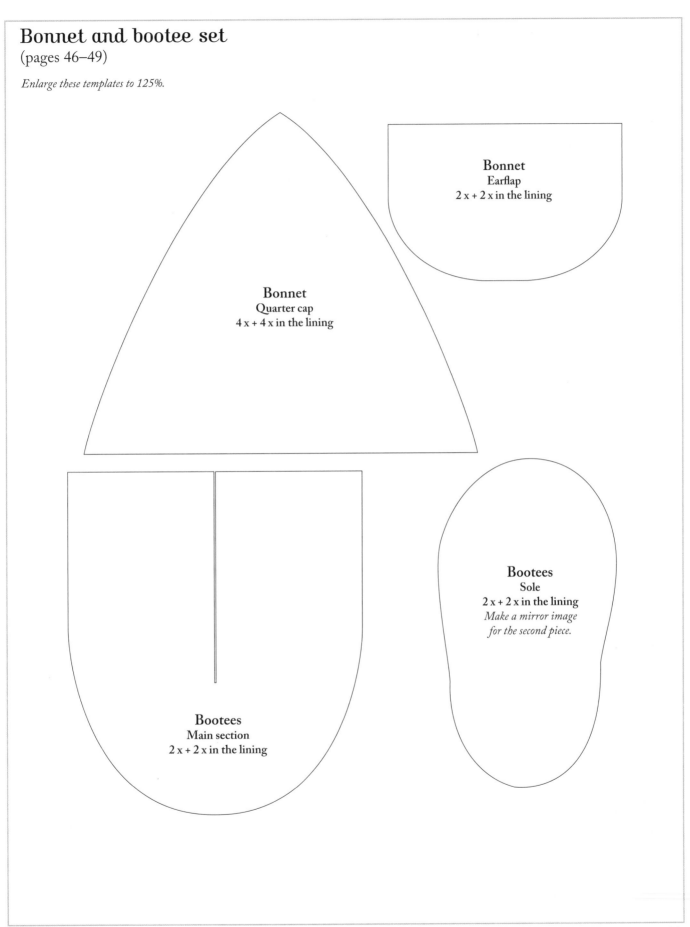

Bonnet
Earflap
2 x + 2 x in the lining

Bonnet
Quarter cap
4 x + 4 x in the lining

Bootees
Sole
2 x + 2 x in the lining
*Make a mirror image
for the second piece.*

Bootees
Main section
2 x + 2 x in the lining

Lily and her basket (pages 36–41)

Enlarge these templates to 125%.

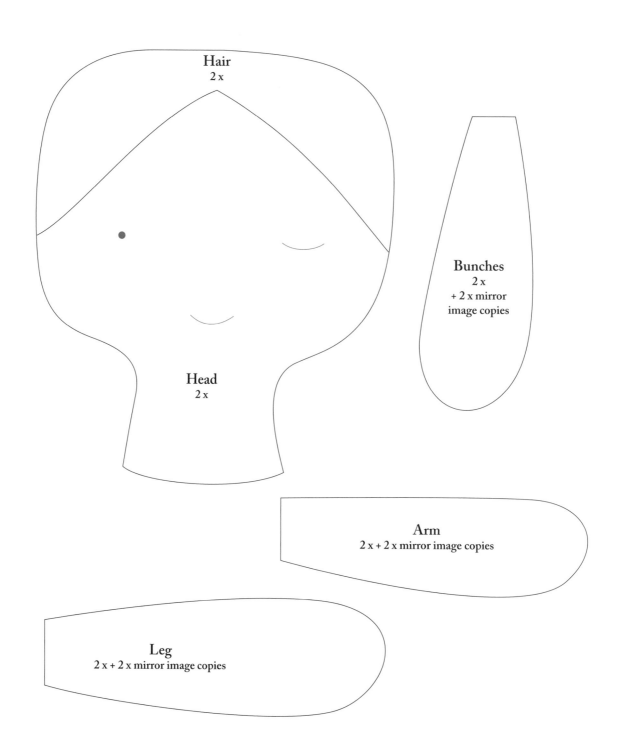

Hair
2 x

Head
2 x

Bunches
2 x
+ 2 x mirror
image copies

Arm
2 x + 2 x mirror image copies

Leg
2 x + 2 x mirror image copies

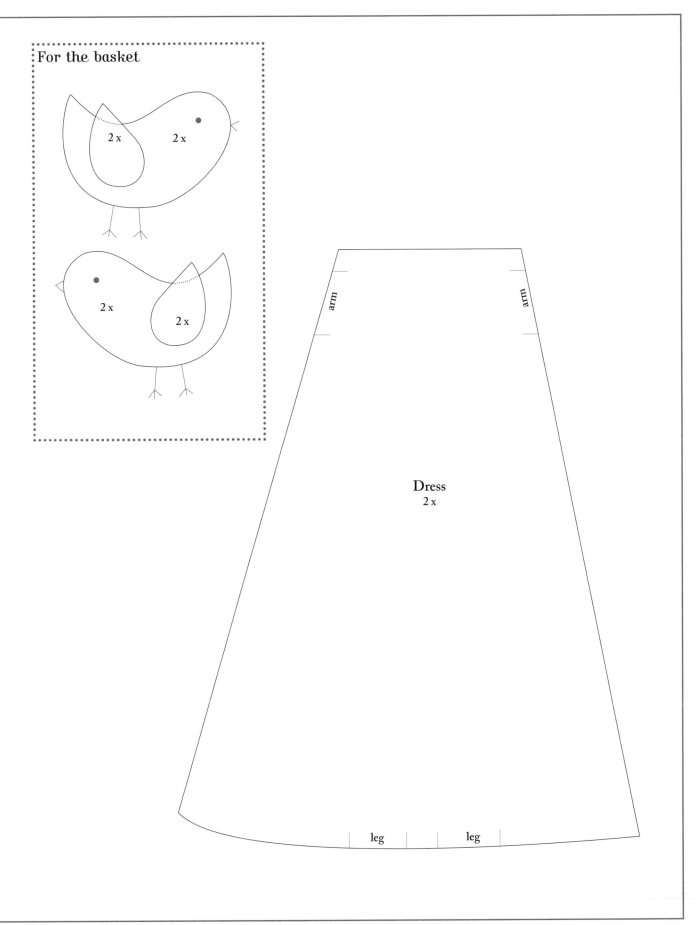

For the basket

2 x   2 x

2 x   2 x

arm   arm

Dress
2 x

leg   leg

Patchwork cot liner
(pages 52–54)

Enlarge this template to 125%.

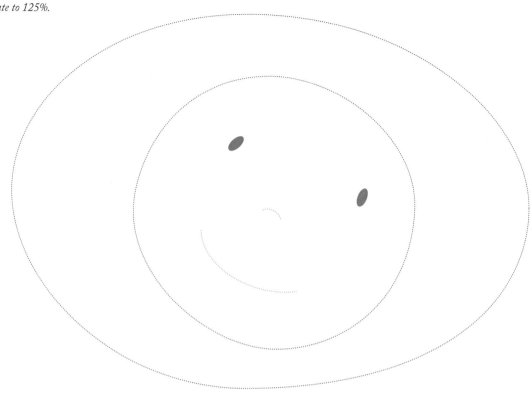

Customized t-shirts (pages 62–63)

Enlarge these templates to 125%.

Book of animals
(pages 68–71)

Enlarge these templates to 125%.

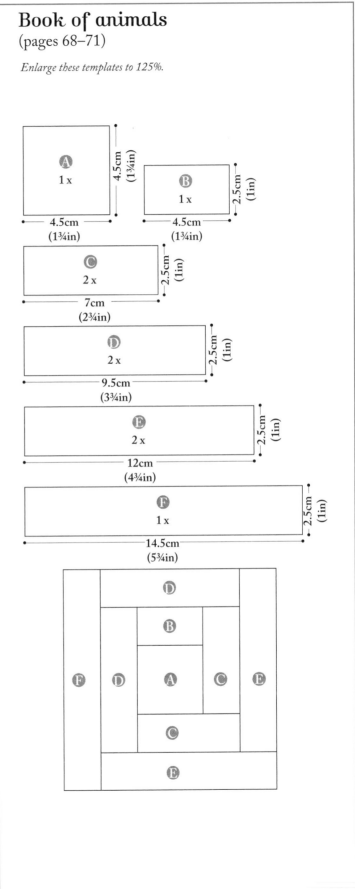

Book of animals (pages 68–71)

Budding artist's pencil case (pages 83–85)
Sketch pouch (pages 86–87)

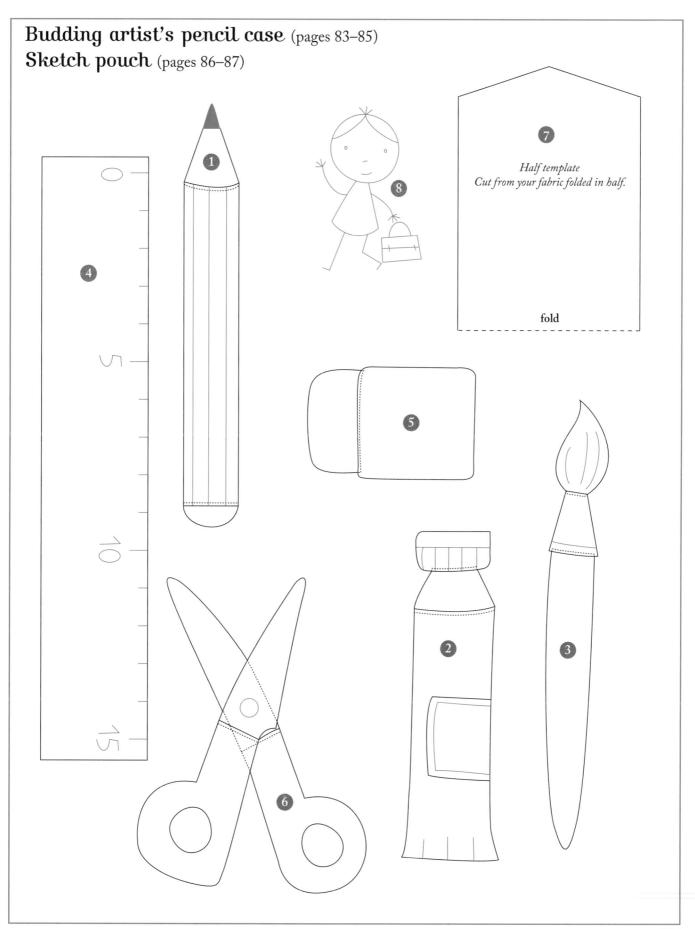

*Half template
Cut from your fabric folded in half.*

fold

Butterfly blanket (pages 58–61)

Enlarge these templates to 125%.

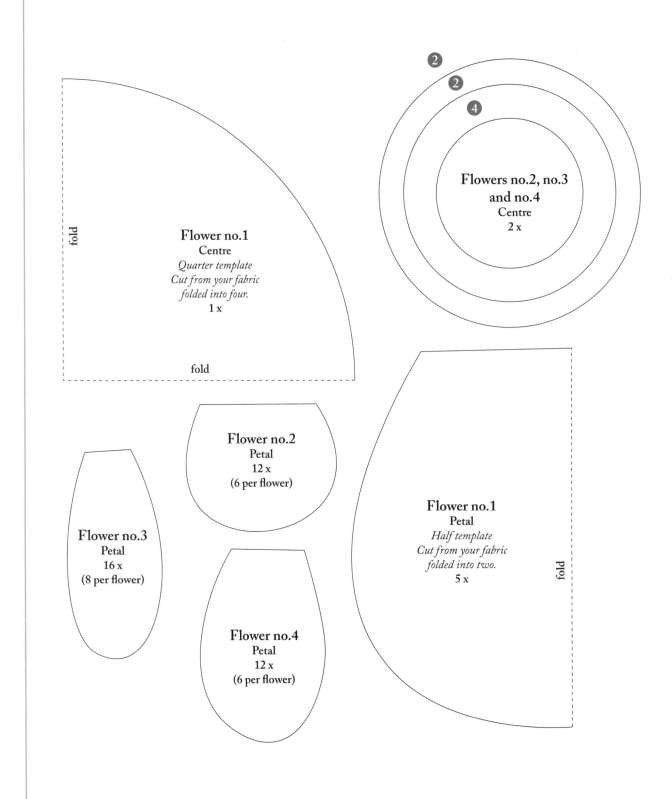

Flower no.1
Centre
*Quarter template
Cut from your fabric
folded into four.*
1 x

fold

fold

**Flowers no.2, no.3
and no.4**
Centre
2 x

Flower no.2
Petal
12 x
(6 per flower)

Flower no.3
Petal
16 x
(8 per flower)

Flower no.4
Petal
12 x
(6 per flower)

Flower no.1
Petal
*Half template
Cut from your fabric
folded into two.*
5 x

fold

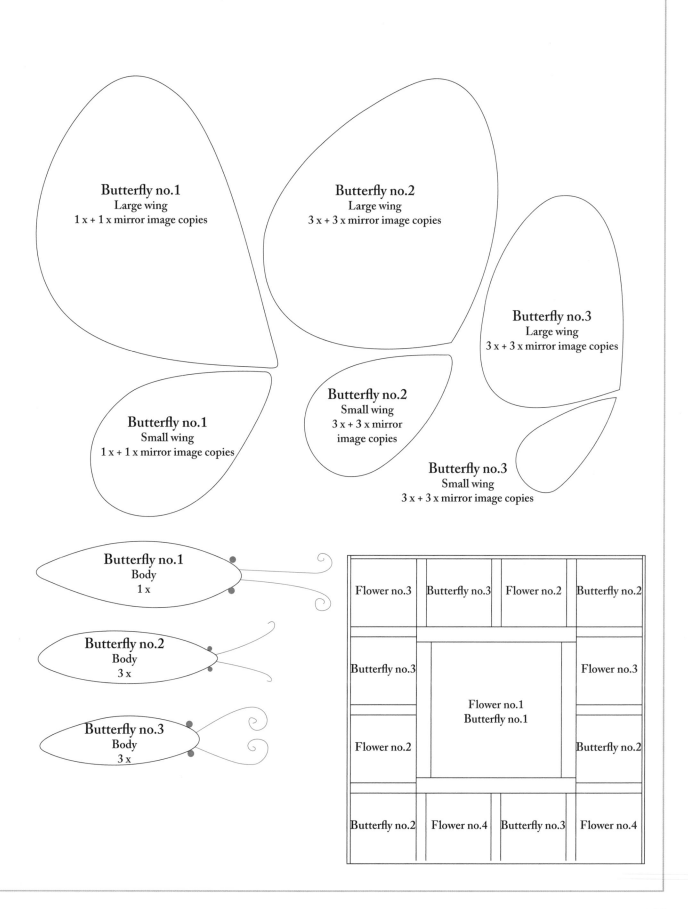

Butterfly no.1
Large wing
1 x + 1 x mirror image copies

Butterfly no.2
Large wing
3 x + 3 x mirror image copies

Butterfly no.3
Large wing
3 x + 3 x mirror image copies

Butterfly no.1
Small wing
1 x + 1 x mirror image copies

Butterfly no.2
Small wing
3 x + 3 x mirror
image copies

Butterfly no.3
Small wing
3 x + 3 x mirror image copies

Butterfly no.1
Body
1 x

Butterfly no.2
Body
3 x

Butterfly no.3
Body
3 x

Flower no.3	Butterfly no.3	Flower no.2	Butterfly no.2
Butterfly no.3			Flower no.3
Flower no.2	Flower no.1 Butterfly no.1		Butterfly no.2
Butterfly no.2	Flower no.4	Butterfly no.3	Flower no.4

Aprons (pages 94–97)

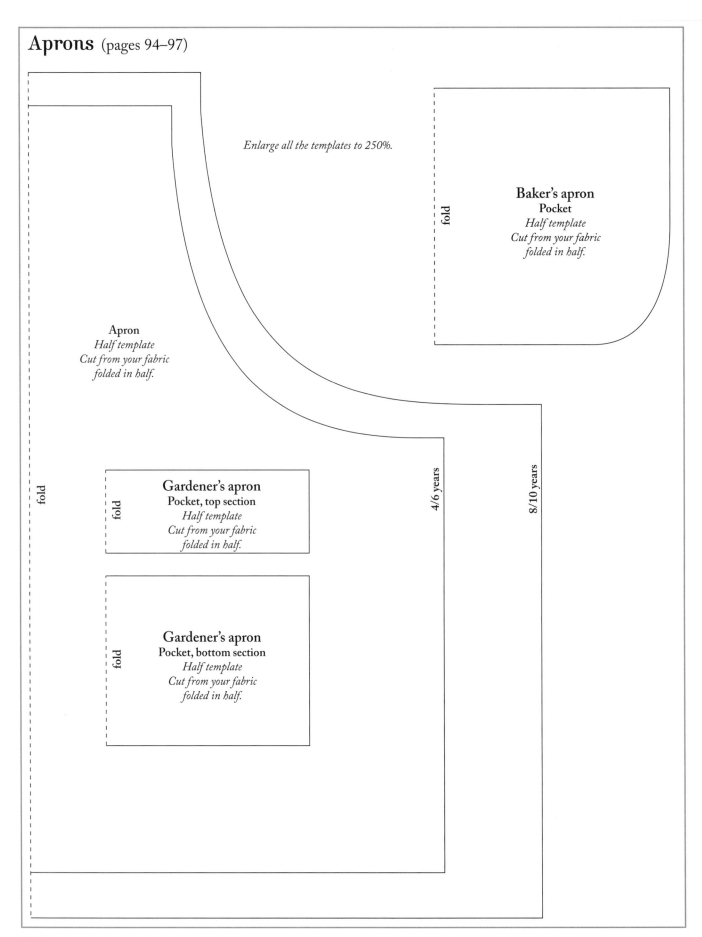

Enlarge all the templates to 250%.

Baker's apron
Pocket
*Half template
Cut from your fabric
folded in half.*

fold

Apron
*Half template
Cut from your fabric
folded in half.*

fold

Gardener's apron
Pocket, top section
*Half template
Cut from your fabric
folded in half.*

fold

Gardener's apron
Pocket, bottom section
*Half template
Cut from your fabric
folded in half.*

fold

4/6 years

8/10 years

Baker's apron (pages 94–95)

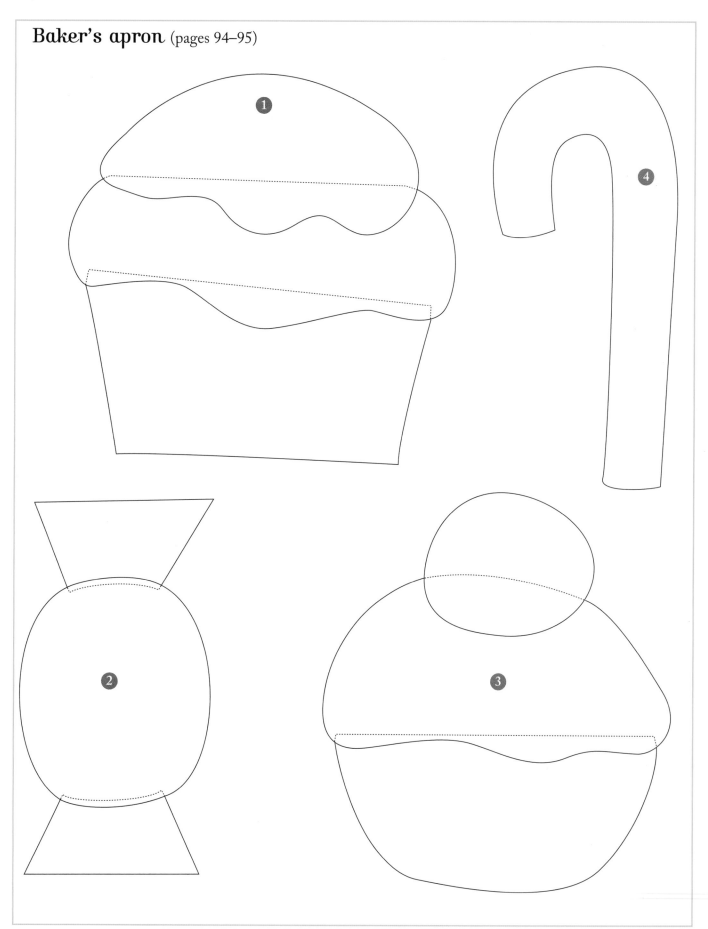

Carry play mat (pages 75–77)

Enlarge these templates to 125%.

My secret case
(pages 26–27)

Enlarge these templates to 125%.

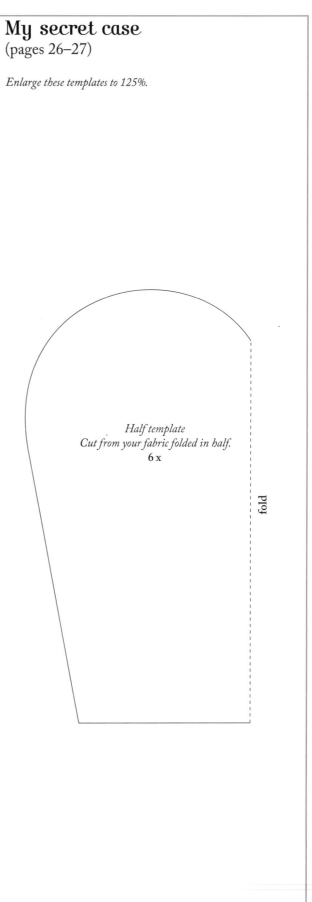

*Half template
Cut from your fabric folded in half.*
6 x

fold

Travel bag (pages 64–66)

Enlarge these templates to 125%.

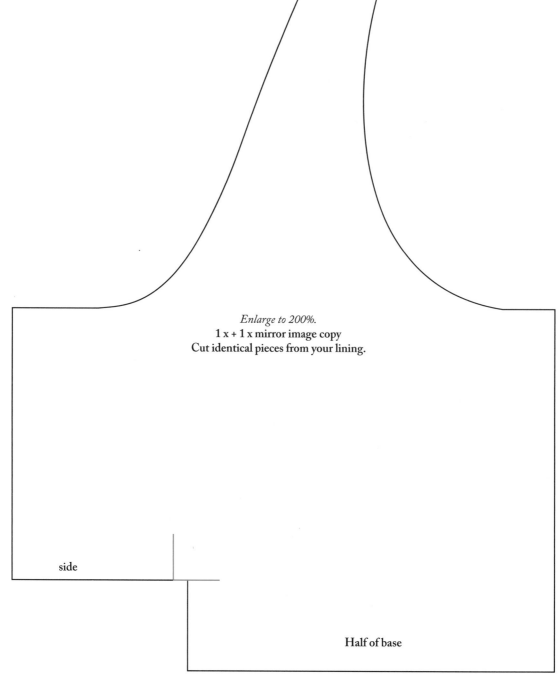

Enlarge to 200%.
1 x + 1 x mirror image copy
Cut identical pieces from your lining.

side

Half of base

Snack bag (pages 88–90)

Enlarge these templates to 125%.

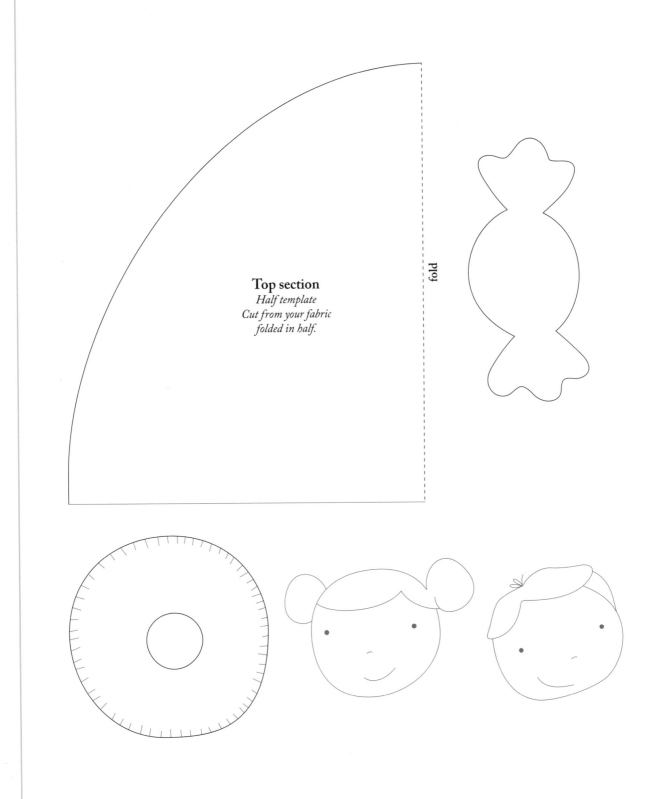

Top section
Half template
Cut from your fabric
folded in half.

fold

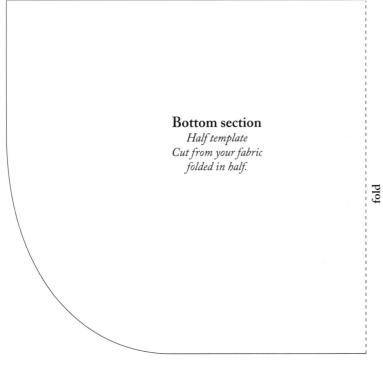

Bottom section
Half template
Cut from your fabric
folded in half.

fold

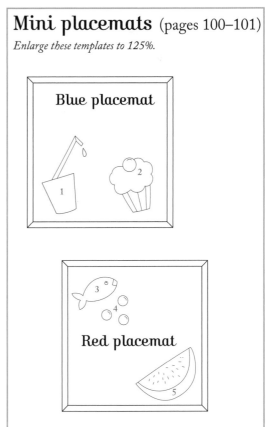

Mini placemats (pages 100–101)

Enlarge these templates to 125%.

Blue placemat

1

2

Red placemat

3

4

5

Colourful bibs (pages 104–105)

Enlarge these templates to 125%.

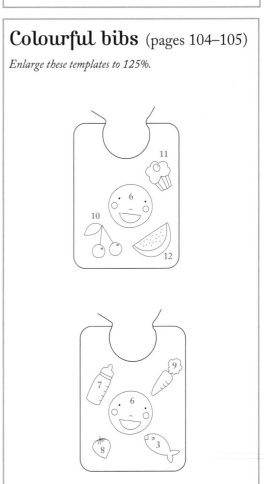

11

6

10

12

7

9

6

8

3

Mini placemats (pages 100–101)
Colourful bibs (pages 104–105)

Enlarge these templates to 125%.

① ⑦ ⑨ ⑥

③

*Make a mirror image
copy for the bib.*

④ 3 x

⑧

⑩

⑤ ②

⑫ ⑪

Sweetie bag (pages 91–93)

Enlarge these templates to 125%.

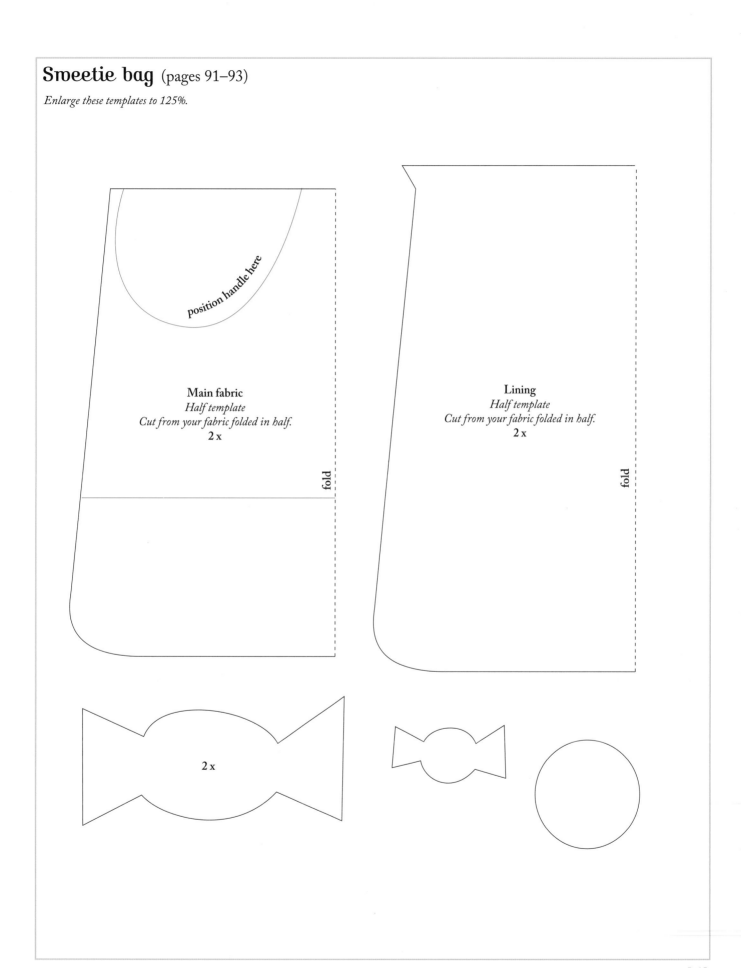

Main fabric
Half template
Cut from your fabric folded in half.
2 x

position handle here

fold

Lining
Half template
Cut from your fabric folded in half.
2 x

fold

2 x

Advent calendar (pages 107–109)

Enlarge these templates to 125%.

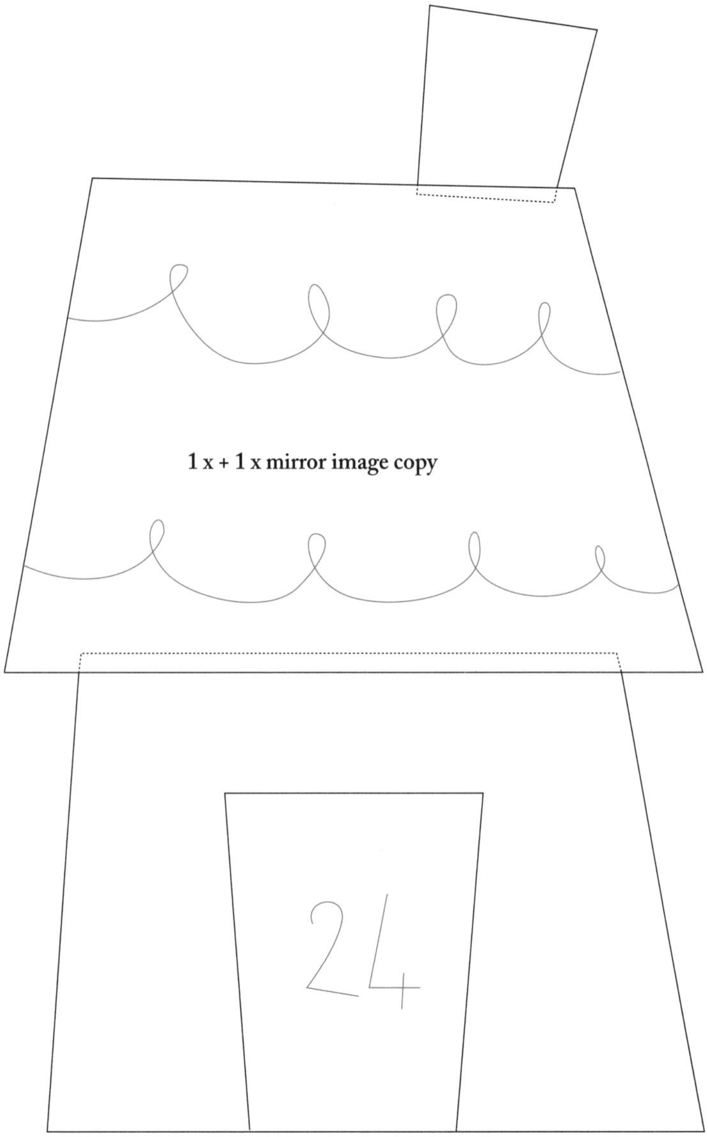

1 x + 1 x mirror image copy

24

1 large Christmas tree
2 small Christmas tree

3 large present
4 medium present
5 small present

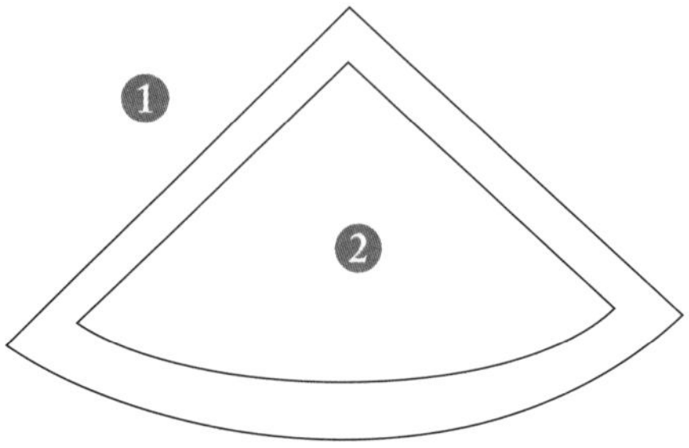

1

2

Napkin cases (pages 102–103)